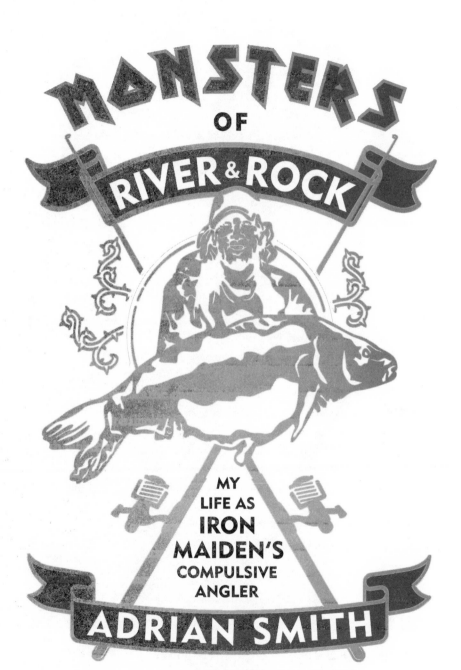

MONSTERS

OF

RIVER & ROCK

MY
LIFE AS
**IRON
MAIDEN'S**
COMPULSIVE
ANGLER

ADRIAN SMITH

BMG

First published by Ebury Publishing, a division of
The Random House Group Ltd.

Cover design and illustration by Two Associates

Back cover photograph and back flap photography by Nathalie Dufresne-Smith

ISBN: 9781947026872
Published by BMG

www.bmg.com

This book is dedicated to my dad.

CONTENTS

Prologue   ix

1   First Lines   1

2   Sunday Morning Sidewalks – My First Carp   7

3   Barbel – From Black And White To Colour   21

4   Battling With The Beast   31

5   A Very Big Chub   41

6   New York, New York – City Rats And
     Largemouth Bass   53

7   Miami – Peacock Bass In The City Of Vice   63

8   A Canadian Adventure – Trout And Bears   77

9   New Zealand And The Monster Of Rock   105

10   A River Twenty   135

11   Pike Fishing And Oasis   143

12   Sturgeon And Falling Over In Vancouver   155

13   Parisienne Carpways   163

14   Tench – Quest For A 'Double'   181

15 Jumbo Jets And Jumbo Tench   201

16 Fishing With Friends And Family   219

17 High Jinks On The Lower Trent   237

18 Bonefish And The Reverend   259

Epilogue   277

Acknowledgements   279

Glossary   281

Index   285

PROLOGUE

It's 7pm and darkness is descending on the streets of Mexico City. I'm sitting directly behind the driver in a van which has seen better days. Up ahead is a police car, siren blaring, blue and red lights flashing. It is trying to carve a route through the late rush-hour traffic so the other members of Iron Maiden and I can make it to the show in time. We alternate between mad, 80mph dashes on the wrong side of the road to lurching, abrupt halts. I begin to feel slightly queasy as the driver slams on the brakes once again as a 'civilian' car, with a driver who hasn't read the script, pulls out in front of us. Our driver is wearing sunglasses. In the dark. He's either forgotten to take them off or, more likely, he's living out some long-held car-chase fantasy. Now we've come to a halt and the driver of the afore- mentioned 'civi' car has got out and tried to punch out one of the cops . . . chaos. This is a police escort: it sounds glamorous, it is anything but . . .

I close my eyes, lean back in my seat and try to block out all the madness. Now in my mind I am by the side of a lake. It is early morning and mist hangs over the water like a ghostly veil. I am fishing. Out on the lake, the dorsal fin of a large tench cuts through the mirror-calm surface, sending out oily ripples in a perfect circle. I bait my hook with two grains of corn, pack the feeder with groundbait and lob the whole lot out 20 yards or so into the lake. With the rod on the rests, I clip on the bobbin, light my stove and put the kettle on for the first tea of the day.

CHAPTER ONE

First Lines

Why do we go fishing? Someone once said (OK, it was Billy Connolly), 'Fishing is like meditation, only with a punchline.' Excitement is not a word most non-fisherfolk would associate with the sport, yet for me it's a key part. Delicious anticipation is a phrase I like. Planning a trip and the build-up puts me in a good mood for weeks beforehand.

The primal need to hunt. I think most men have an instinct to put food on the table, whether it's a guy earning a living in a high-powered job or simply someone dangling a worm, trying to catch his supper. You can try to rationalise it all you want, but I suppose I go fishing because I just love it. Clapton, where I grew up in east London, was not exactly a place of babbling brooks and pristine lakes. We did have the Lee Navigation, a canal river, running down the bottom of our road. Perfect, you might say. Unfortunately not. On a summer's day you could smell the river – a sickly perfumed aroma – a mile away, such were the levels of industrial pollution in the waterway.

This didn't stop curious kids though. The Lea was bordered on one side by factories and on the other by Hackney Marshes. The marshes might as well have been called 'The Forbidden Lands' as far as I was concerned. My mother was always telling me, with pointed finger, 'You're not to go over the Marshes!' Of course, being a fairly normal eight-year-old boy, I'd be over there all the time. My brave mates and I would be on 'full alert' the whole time, as those badlands were roamed by all sorts of thieves and vagabonds.

Hackney Marshes were, though, an oasis in an urban jungle. It covered about five square miles of green marshland before you got to the famous football pitches (there are dozens of them, laid out in a grid). There were a couple of ponds or 'bomb craters', as the area had been heavily bombed during the Second World War. We plundered these for newts and sticklebacks. I remember one day marvelling at the sight of a kestrel hovering above the marsh. For a lad who was only used to sparrows and bedraggled starlings in our little back garden, this was truly an incredible sight. The bird above might as well have been a pterodactyl.

The marsh was bordered by the Coppermill Stream and Walthamstow reservoirs. The Coppermill ran for around two miles from one of the reservoirs, before joining the River Lea opposite Springfield Park in Clapton. Of course, this was another no-go area, cut off from curious boys by an eight-foot-high fence, but by taking a running jump and clambering up, you could hang on and get a glimpse of the river on the other side. The stream was usually clear and, if you were lucky, you would see a shoal of big roach or bream holding in the current between the swaying fronds of weed. I would hang on to the top of the fence until my sinews strained and my mates drifted off to more exciting pursuits, like walking on the railway line. They say forbidden fruit tastes sweeter. Perhaps the fact that these no-go areas were attractive to me is why I still have a deep appreciation and respect for the countryside.

My dad Fred, like a lot of working-class men, worked hard all week and looked forward to his fishing on Sunday. He started to take me as soon as I could hold a fishing rod. He, my older brother Patrick and myself would go to the Grand Union Canal on the gasworks stretch (yes, it was as grim as it sounds), usually on a Sunday afternoon. I fished happily for the eager, small perch, while Dad patiently fed his swim with hempseed before slowly building a netful of 'goer roach'. The day would end with him letting me 'poach' his swim and being rewarded with a beautiful, silver roach, red fins sparkling, a stark contrast to the glowering spectre of the gasworks opposite. Who knew such beauty could exist in such harsh surroundings? Certainly not the people going about their business on the street that backed onto the canal. We would enter and exit it via a gap in the railings (why were all my favourite places fenced off?), even though my dad had all the London Anglers' Association permits. We would trudge, laden with tackle, back to the car conveniently parked near the pub. My dad would pop in 'for a quick one' and I would wait for him on the boozer's step, happily munching crisps and guzzling lemonade, or ginger wine in winter.

Sometimes, music would start up in the pub and, on sticking my head through the door, I'd see my dad up on the small stage. In those days, most public houses had a resident pianist and Dad liked nothing better than getting up with him and singing a few songs. Sinatra, Perry Como and Dean Martin would form the bulk of his 'set'. He had a pretty good voice and, whenever he walked into his local, the regulars would always call out, 'Gorn, Freddy, give us a song, son!' After a few pints of beer he would usually oblige. It used to surprise me at first, because he was quite a shy man, but perhaps that was the point. Music was important to him, enough to overcome any inhibitions and get up on the stage. I can relate to that. He also played the ukulele and accordion before he badly damaged a hand in an accident at work.

My mother, Kathleen, also loved music. Born in County Mayo, Ireland, she was taught to read music and play the violin from an early age. She always broke out the fiddle at parties, and could pretty much play anything. Her real joy, though, was traditional Irish folk music. She knew loads of jigs and reels. Most of them had funny names like 'Mrs O'Reilly's Kitchen'. Or maybe it was 'Mrs O'Reilly's Chicken'. Once, when I was very young, I went to the cupboard where she kept the fiddle and, intrigued, I started to try and play it. She must have heard my screeching and scratching, because before long I heard the sound of urgent footsteps coming down the hall. Panicking, I quickly shoved the instrument back into the cupboard. In my haste, I slammed the door on the fragile neck of the violin, breaking off the headstock in the process. Mum was not pleased.

The only other place we fished around that time, apart from the Grand Union Canal, was Tottenham Locks on the Lee Navigation. The river from Tottenham right down to its confluence with the Thames at Three Mills was little more than an open sewer. Above the lock, however, the water was clean enough to support life. Loads of willing gudgeon for me, and plenty of my dad's beloved roach. The river here was wide and windswept, the fish small, but scenically it was a step up from the 'Cut'.

I still didn't have the required patience to fish for the roach and couldn't wait to feverishly start snatching bleak and hapless gudgeon, much to the disgust of my dad. He would sit, heron-like, a huge bamboo pole extended out into 'the boat road' or canal middle, an antenna float dotted down for maximum sensitivity. After an hour of inactivity, I would hear him almost whisper, 'Just 'ad a bite, boy.'

So, my love of fishing grew, and I suppose music was already in my blood. Mind you, I can't say I was thinking of Mrs O'Reilly or Perry Como when I wrote 'Wasted Years' . . .

CHAPTER TWO

Sunday Morning Sidewalks

My First Carp

Carp. The king of English coarse fish. The biggest, hardest fighting and arguably – in the case of mirror carp – the most handsome. Today they are widespread and even if you are a novice, you can go to numerous heavily stocked ponds and catch your first double-figure carp – weighing over 10lb – or 20-pounder. Not so when I was starting out fishing, many years ago. The carp then was a rare creature, mythical and considered almost uncatchable.

Friday night in the early 1970s took on a routine for me. When darkness fell, I would be out collecting lobworms or nightcrawlers by torchlight. On Saturday morning, armed with a few dozen juicy lobs, I would hotfoot it over to my waiting customer, John Barry, who would buy them off me for a few bob. John and his dad were a rare breed in those days – some called them specimen hunters or carp nuts. They were among a small band of hardy anglers that camped by the water and fished all night. Nowadays such tactics are the norm, but then it was regarded as extreme. 'Fanatics', my dad called them, like they were a sort of piscatorial terrorist group, but they certainly fired my imagination. It was rumoured that one of the group had caught a mirror carp of 12lb! A very respectable weight at the time.

It's amazing to think that, now, almost anyone can go to one of the heavily stocked pools and catch carp of that size, all day long. Things change. Now you can record an album on your laptop using digital sounds. Said album can be sold via your own website, publicised on Instagram, with videos shown on Facebook. Too easy? After all, isn't it all about the journey, the struggle? Doesn't the effort involved make the achievement worthwhile? Maybe. I think it's a case of relative reality.

The waters John and his dad fished were known as 'The Pits', run by the now defunct Abbotts Angling Society near the village of Stanstead Abbotts in Hertfordshire. The Pits were dug out for sand and gravel in the 1950s. By the mid-1960s the holes in the ground had been flooded by the River Lea to form several lakes, and the whole site had matured with willow trees and sedge beds lining the banks. The 'Abbotts' had taken on the fishing rights and my dad had bought permits for himself, my brother Patrick and me. I treasured Sundays 'over the Pits', and it was a lush oasis compared with Tottenham Locks and the inner-city Grand Union Canal.

A typical Sunday would see us up at first light and driving to Stanstead Abbotts from Clapton. Up to Stamford Hill, down St Anne's Road, past my school, St Ignatius Primary. We would pick up the old Cambridge Road, continuing on through Edmonton and Enfield, the streets deserted, Sunday morning sidewalks in the blue-pink light of the early day. The concrete sprawl would fall away as we entered Cheshunt, Broxbourne and Hoddesdon. Forgive my misty-eyed nostalgia. Those memories are worth savouring, as now those once pleasant country towns consist mainly of spiteful one-way systems, bland grey business parks and bustling crowds. No doubt more prosperous. Better? Mm . . .

Sometimes we wouldn't set out until Sunday lunchtime as my dad often worked the mornings, finishing off a job some-where. This had its benefits, though, as he did enjoy a lunchtime pint. This would usually mean stopping at the Queen's Head at the top of Marsh Lane in Stanstead Abbotts. As a boy, I'd get a shandy and crisps outside while I waited for Dad, but at 14 or 15 I could be smuggled into the pub itself for a half of lager. *Ah, a man at last*, I thought, sitting with Dad having a beer, not realising the journey had just begun.

Inspired by the exploits of John Barry and his crew, and my newfound manliness, I decided I would spend the next trip to the Pits trying to catch a carp. So, instead of tying the usual 2½lb hook length and 16-hook-and-maggot perch-bashing combo, I changed tack. I attached a size 8 hook, which I had scrounged from the debris-filled bottom of Dad's fishing bag, direct to my 4lb reel line. I had also just inherited my brother's Apollo Taperflash hollow steel rod, him having given up fishing for reasons I could not understand. Mind you, he had caught a 3lb common a few seasons earlier from one of the Pits, on a 'roach pole' to boot! Perhaps it was burnout, too much too young. A case of 'I'll never top that.'

By this time, Dad and I didn't always fish side by side and he let me wander off to explore on my own. I'd found a tasty-looking swim. It was set on a spit of land that jutted out into the pit. From this position it was a short chuck to a gravel plateau crowned with a stand of sedges.

Two big lobworms were placed on the hook, with an Arlesey Bomb (cutting-edge technology at the time) placed a foot above the end tackle, held in place by a split shot. As I was using a centrepin, another of bruv's hand-me-downs, the line was pulled off the reel with my left hand. By gathering the line loops between the bottom three rings, then swinging the rod gently sideways and forwards, it was possible to cast a fair distance. The worms plopped down perfectly, six inches from the reeds in about two feet of water. The rod was placed in two rests, and a silver foil bobbin was made from my sandwich wrapping. I sat well back from the water's edge, remembering that carp were clever, wily, and I was a specimen hunter!

It was a totally different feeling. Usually by this time I'd half-filled my keepnet with stunned roach and perch but now, here I was with my stall set out. Big fish or bust. I felt more than slightly fearful. I'd never, up to that point, caught anything bigger than a half-pound roach. What if I did hook a carp? This was a new feeling: adrenalin, the buzz. I was utterly absorbed . . .

As often happens, the take came out of the blue. The foil hit the butt, the poor old centrepin whined and the rod hooped round as something made off with the worms. My mind was reeling (pardon the pun). I was going to land a carp, gain the respect of other anglers, my dad. I'd be in the *Angling Times* maybe! Pints all round in the pub. Dad might even let me smoke. The fish might even be bigger than my brother's!

I grabbed the rod and tried to stop the fish as the rod buckled, and the carp, for I had no doubt now that's what it was, powered off across the pit.

Then the line broke. As did my heart. The silence was deafening as I watched the line hanging limply from the rod-tip. The carp disappeared into the depths, along with my dreams. In my excitement I'd tried to stop the fish instead of letting it run, clamping my hand on the spinning reel. A classic rookie mistake. And God knows how old that line was on the centrepin.

That was the last time I fished the Pits – or anywhere for that matter – seriously for the next ten years. That summer around 1972 or '73 singled the end of my childhood years. My parents and careers officers at school were all asking the same question: 'What are you going to do with your life when you leave school?' The big question that faces everyone. Like most 15-year-olds, I hadn't a clue. I'd never been interested in the academic side of school life, coasting through lessons until it was time for sports, well, football. I had been a Manchester United fan since I could remember. They were the days of George Best, my idol, Law and Charlton. Like most young boys, I had dreamed of becoming a footballer. I played for the school team and, when I was around ten or eleven years old, I was sent along with another boy called Doug D'Cruz for a trial with the Haringey Borough team, or Tottenham Boys as they were known. On a bright autumn day, my brother Patrick took me down to the trial on a vast windswept pitch somewhere in north London.

The game was a bit of a blur. It seemed like there were about 50 hopefuls competing for the attention of the coaches. No time, no space . . . I was desperate to impress, of course. But, according to my bro, my performance was restricted to a couple of head-down dribbles, then losing the ball. Oh, for some coaching! The game was over before I knew it. The coaches had seen enough and the fresh-faced fourth-years were lined up for selection. Dreams still intact at that point . . .

The men lined up, notepapers on clipboards, rattling and fluttering in the gusty wind as they prepared to call out the names of the future stars.

The names were called, the list growing, but still no mention. Then it was over. The coaches thanked everyone. Goodbye. I hadn't been chosen, nor had Doug. Ouch. I felt hugely disappointed, and slightly embarrassed. If life was a game of footy, I had just been booted into row Z by a burly defender! An early lesson, but perhaps a bit hard for a ten-year-old. Looking back, if I'd had real ambition, or real ability for that matter, I would have kept trying. As it was, I kept playing for another three or four years, then stopped. Maybe it was one too many freezing rain-lashed mornings on the battlegrounds of Hackney Marshes football pitches against boys stronger and more determined than me.

At around 15 years old, feeling lost and clueless, moping around the house one day, I wandered into my older sister Kathleen's room. She had a record player and I would go and look at her records from time to time. The Temptations, Marvin Gaye, Percy Sledge, Deep Purple. Deep Purple, eh? What's this? This was not her usual taste. I picked up the album. I must have looked like Neanderthal man discovering fire for the first time: curious, a bit wary. The album was called *Machine Head*. I removed the record from the sleeve and placed it on the turntable. 'Highway Star'. The song built slowly, a burning fuse, Ian Gillan's primal yet musical scream leading the band into what would be the chugging anthem to my teens. Ahh . . . this is what I want to do!

Fishing took a back seat, although I still had a permit to fish the Pits and I went occasionally, usually with a girlfriend. This was little more than a ruse on my part, though, and I spent more time fumbling around with bra straps and buttons than trying to

13

catch fish. Like my early fishing exploits, this usually led to tangles and frustration. My dad, who had taught me how to tie a spade-end hook and handle a roach pole, hadn't taught me much about the opposite sex. I'm still learning.

Unknown to me, around that time another boy was going through the same process. Dave Murray grew up a few streets over from me, in Clapton, but we had never met. We were introduced by a mutual friend, Dave McLaughlin. The two Daves were a little further along the road to stardom than me. Both owned and could play electric guitars. Wow! Not only this, they also worked together at De Havilland's shoe factory in Homerton. This meant they looked the part as well. They always had the latest platform boots in fashionably gaudy colours, albeit supposed 'seconds' – 'The buffer slipped, honest, guv.' They were also the only other lads with long hair in the neighbourhood. With our shared love of music we naturally gravitated towards each other and were regarded as hippies or freaks, which suited us fine! I used to stroll about in a full-length fur coat, bright blue loon trousers and a bobble hat. This, remember, was not Hollywood or Hampstead, but in east London where everyone was supposed to conform and couldn't afford to do otherwise. You left school early, got a job to help pay family bills, and had a steady 'bird' or girlfriend. When old enough to drive, you'd buy a car, preferably a flashy, noisy one where you and Tracey or Dawn would drive around the streets. If you weren't 'hard' you certainly had to act as if you were. God forbid you showed any weakness. The years would pass, marriage, kids, work, until one day you'd end up spent at 60, coughing your guts up in the pub after another cigarette and too much beer. All done to the tune of 'My Way'. It didn't appeal to me one bit, so that was motivation sorted.

I always thought I would be happy just making a living playing music. I didn't have lofty ambitions to be a rock star. I looked at it like an apprenticeship: learn your instrument, your craft, and maybe you could make a living. Having said that, I couldn't help imagining what it would be like to be in a big band, and have fame and fortune . . .

It was sometime in 1972 that the two Daves and I met up at Dave Murray's house with the idea of playing some music together. I had told them I was a singer, despite the fact that, apart from a talent contest at a holiday camp when I was about ten, I had never sang in my life before. I had a microphone, though, which I had begged my parents to buy me for Christmas in anticipation of meeting up with the 'Daves'. The fact that I actually owned a mic convinced the chaps to give me a try.

Singing, I thought, would give me an 'in' with these two cool dudes without actually having to learn an instrument. I wanted to be in a 'band', I didn't want to worry about trifles such as actually being able to play.

Dave Murray owned an amplifier and, luckily, it had multiple inputs enabling us to plug in both guitars and my microphone. Not exactly state-of-the-art.

'What we gonna play?' said Dave Mac.

'D'you know "Silver Machine"?' I asked. Hawkwind's song was riding high in the charts at the time. I watched Dave Murray place his hand on the fretboard of his EROS SG copy in the barre chord position and he counted off, 'Na Na Na, Na Na Na, Na Na Na' etc. He played the four-chord sequence perfectly and I felt the thrill of a loud, clear, electric guitar for the first time. He could play! I was impressed. Dave Mac joined in and both guitarists cued me in for the vocal. I had no idea what was going to come out of my mouth. I was a pretty shy kid but I thought, *Well, this is it. No time to be bashful.*

'I . . . I just took a ride,' I bellowed into the mic, 'in a silver machine . . . and I'm still feeling mean!'

The lone speaker in Dave's little amp farted and growled in protest but there was no doubt, something resembling music was being produced. We finished the song.

'D'you know "Whiskey in the Jar"?' said someone excitedly. Off we went, Dave Mac singing this time, a little more restrained and melodic than my 'shouty' style, and Dave Murray was playing the solo note for note. The characteristic smooth-neck pickup sound was there already. Next up Chuck Berry's 'Johnny B. Goode', Dave knocking off the intro like a pro, and me back on vocals. I was dizzy. We were a band! Before we called it a day, I asked Dave to show me some chords. He demonstrated the barre chord A (as in 'Silver Machine'), and then handed me another guitar that had been standing in the corner. Wow! It was a Woolworth's job, a spiteful red colour with a finger-shreddingly high action. I gritted my teeth and pressed down the strings in the position Dave was showing me. Pain shot through my fingers but I clamped down. I would master this chord, for I had already worked out that if the chord shape was moved up and down the neck, the A became A, B, C, D, etc. (It was only after playing for two years that I went back and learned open chords.) Dave said the guitar was for sale for the sum of £5. I had to have it. I was back the next day with the money after promising my dad that I would help him out at work for a couple of days.

So the weekly music paper the *Melody Maker* replaced the *Angling Times* as my read of choice, and Black Sabbath, Free and Purple replaced George Best and Manchester United. The next ten years were spent chasing the dream of being a professional musician, and such childish things as footie and fishing were cast aside.

Looking at the moody Ritchie Blackmore and Paul Kossoff, my new heroes, I couldn't imagine them doing anything but practising guitar and fighting off adoring female fans. Ritchie trotting down for roach? Kossoff employing the floating-crust method for carp? Never! From now on, I decided, I would dedicate my life to music. Everything else was uncool. I left school at 15 with this vague but heartfelt notion. At the bottom of the employment food chain, I performed a number of dead-end jobs including being a milkman, office boy and cushion stuffer! At least I had an income and I eventually saved enough to buy my first 'proper' guitar. It was a Gibson Les Paul Gold Top for £235; the result of a summer spent working on a building site. I still have that guitar and use it for work today.

Ironically it was joining Iron Maiden that relit the fishing fire once more. Drummer and roommate in those days was

Clive Burr, a keen angler, and Dave Murray who also liked an occasional 'dabble', so days off on tour were usually spent trying to find somewhere for the three of us to go fishing.

It was on one of those days in Alpine Valley, Wisconsin, that I caught my first-ever carp. Up to that point, I hadn't even known carp were present in the United States. We were at that time touring the States opening for the Scorpions, supporting our latest album *The Number of the Beast*. We had a day off in Alpine Valley and the hotel grounds backed on to a small river. Clive and I checked out the creek. It looked pretty good, narrow but quite deep. It had a strong flow but a few tasty-looking eddies and pools. But, was fishing allowed?

'Fishing? In our little ol' creek?' said the lady at the front desk. 'Well, ya can if ya want but there's nothin' in there but a bunch of dirty big ol' carp!' she exclaimed. At the time, the carp was regarded as a 'trash' fish in the US. Nowadays, thanks to people like ex-pat Wayne Boon and organisations like the American Carp Society, people are affording more respect to the species. Anyway, hearing there were carp present in the creek was music to the ears of us English boys abroad.

Clive, Dave and I set off to Sears department store as we hadn't brought any fishing gear with us. In the great American tradition, Sears was the original superstore. You could buy anything – from candyfloss to automatic rifles, and everything in between. We managed to pick up some gear, though the bass rods we bought seemed quite puny compared to the stuff we used back home. In fact, they were those all-in-one 'fishing set' rod and reel combos that come in a flimsy plastic case. The close-faced reel contained some robust-looking line, though. You could have towed a barge with it.

Equipped with our new tackle, we headed off to the creek. I settled down in a nice slack area off the main flow. Clive and Dave headed off downstream. By this time it was early afternoon. The July sun was high in the sky and the Midwest was in the grip of a heatwave. As it was the day before the show, the odd punter had started to arrive (the hotel was right next to the gig). I'd managed to get hold of some hamburger meat and thought this would be as good a bait as any for the Yankee carp.

The set-up was simplicity itself. The clothesline-like line was threaded through the rings of the bass rod (all four feet of it). Attached was a large hook baited with burger ('Would you like fries with that, sir?'); weight was a drilled bullet. This lot was chucked out into the deep slack and the rod laid on the ground.

The hours passed and the sun blazed down on the three pale English boys. I heard a rustling behind me.

'Ah, you are fishing! Are you going to eat zem?'

I turned around to see Klaus Meine and Rudolf Schenker from the Scorpions. It was a long time ago, but I swear Rudolf was wearing leather trousers despite the raging heat.

'Well, I won't catch much with you two standing there in all your stage gear,' I quipped. 'You'll scare them off!'

Suitably reprimanded, the two Scorpions scuttled away, tails between their legs.

Just then the line twitched. Slowly the slack between the rod top and water tightened. A bite at last! I struck, the rod hooped over and the battle was joined. I still didn't quite believe it was a carp. The carp, the stuff of English legend, estate lakes, Dick Walker, uncatchable . . . But a carp it was and a perfectly conditioned double-figure common lay wallowing on the surface in front of me. In the absence of a landing net, I managed to beach the fish. By this time, a bit of a crowd had gathered. Assorted rock fans and returning Scorpions had taken an interest in my catch. So there I was, my first carp landed, ten years after the disappointment of my lost fish at the Pits, in circumstances I could never have imagined all those years ago.

CHAPTER THREE

Barbel

From Black And White to Colour

My first encounter with a barbel was on a trip with my dad when I was about 13. We had decided on an impromptu visit to the famous Hampshire Avon. For those non-anglers, the River Avon is to barbel and barbel anglers what Wembley is to football fans: hallowed ground. I could barely sleep before the trip such was my level of excitement. I'd never seen a barbel or a big chub, let alone fished for them. I'd heard tales of the Avon's legendary giants. These stories would often be played out on the fishing club's coach outings. Here, usually along with another couple of lads, I would strain to hear the men talking of the fish of the Stour, Wensum or Avon. Of course, the stories would be exaggerated on each subsequent trip; the fish would grow larger, the conditions of capture more extreme, the angler's feat more impressive . . .

Being young and inexperienced, I didn't dare contribute to the conversation. Rather, I just inhaled it, along with gales of hand-rolled cigarette smoke. Sometimes the stories would take on a more colourful tone. There was one angler at the club, Ron, who was quite a successful barbel fisherman. He was also thought to be over-serious in his pursuit. I can still picture him now, perched over his rod on the riverbank, eyes fixated on its tip, roll-up seemingly surgically attached to his lower lip. All working-class men had dangling cigarettes in those days. Perhaps it was the reverse of being 'born with a silver spoon in your mouth'. Ron's obsessiveness didn't go unnoticed by the less successful anglers like Tom, a notorious practical joker. He was elected to take Ron down a peg or two. He was also the possessor of an impressive 'todger', shall we say? On the next fishing trip, Tom crept up on Ron, who was seemingly even more concentrated on his fishing than usual, and there, while his onlooking gallery stifled their giggles, he laid his appendage on Ron's shoulder.

'Any luck, Ron?' somebody said.

'No mate, not yet,' replied Ron, still intent on his rod tip.

More giggles, then a torrent of laughs as poor Ron eventually turned his head to see a very different kind of tackle! I suppose the moral of the story is, there is more to fishing than just fishing.

As it turned out, Dad and I were ill-equipped for the deep, weedy and fast-flowing Avon. We only had our usual match-style tackle and we couldn't hold bottom long enough to stand much of a chance. Dad did manage a decent chub and I a tiny barbel and some small trout, but our flimsy tackle was no match for the mighty River Avon. I did see my first proper barbel, though. Making our way along the bank that morning we encountered another angler. Eager to find out how he was faring, I approached him a little too enthusiastically, only to be told in no uncertain terms to keep away. The angler was long trotting a run, close to the near bank, and I was in danger of blowing his swim. We continued on, with Dad muttering that he was a grumpy so-and-so. The chap must have felt guilty about telling me off because he came up to talk to us later that day. After the usual fishing banter about the weather, water levels, 'you should have been here last week', etc., he told us he had caught a nice barbel and did I want to see it? Not only that, he would take a picture of me holding it. He was obviously some kind of specimen hunter as he had an expensive-looking camera. Even at that tender age, I felt like a bit of a fraud posing with a fish I didn't catch myself, but pose I did. I suppose the fish weighed about 5 or 6lb. I can still remember the unique feel of the barbel, full of wiry, muscular power. It's somehow a noble fish, and barbel anglers, believe it or not, have a great respect for their quarry. They are a strong fish and take the bait violently, wrenching the rod round and fighting harder pound for pound than any coarse fish in the UK, except maybe the carp. They are also not as widespread as most other fish, such as roach, perch and bream, because of their need for fast-flowing, clean water. I didn't know it at the time, but the fish I held in the picture at 13 years old was to be the last one I would see for a little while. A lot would happen to me in those intervening years. Not least becoming a husband and father and having a successful music career.

Sometimes you just get a bee in your bonnet about something. In 1994 I was in the middle of my hiatus from Iron Maiden, which began in 1990. I was dabbling in a few music projects and I had three young children, which is how I got into impromptu short fishing sessions, usually on the River Colne in south Buckinghamshire, near my home. You could always guarantee a few decent chub in the hours either side of darkness, and I did these chub sessions rather than any other type of fishing almost exclusively for a couple of years. I am also a keen reader, and of course angling figures largely in my choice of books. One book I was into at the time was *Big Fish Angling* by Tony Miles. I loved his accounts of fishing for large fish of most species but particularly barbel. It was this and the reports of big barbel in the angling press that really inspired me to have a proper go for them. Where to fish? My local river was reputed to hold them but I felt that on the stretches I fished they were few and far between. Surely I would have picked them up during my chub sessions?

Boyer Leisure, one of the local clubs, had just acquired a stretch of the River Kennet in Berkshire. It was on the opposite bank to the famous Aldermaston Mill stretch and apparently held loads of barbel. I purchased a ticket and read all I could about the Kennet and its inhabitants. Pre-internet, this involved reading more books and pumping the local angling shop assistants and customers for information. The thing about gathering information is, if an angler has had a good fish, you can bet no matter how much he tries to keep it to himself, he's bursting to tell someone. I know, I've done it myself. It's ego, pure and simple, and you usually kick yourself afterwards for letting the cat (or carp) out of the bag. There's also a bit of etiquette involved. When someone is cool and gives you a useful piece of information, you might, after consideration, also offer them a snippet. These nuggets have to be sifted through to find the grains of truth, and the said angler has to be graded. For instance, while mooching around in my local tackle shop, I might hear two anglers similarly mooching, having a quiet chat about a productive stretch of river or the location of a capture of a large fish. This is more likely to contain fact, because it involves minimal bragging. On the other hand, you can go to tackle shops on a Saturday morning and see the angling equivalent of Speakers' Corner. The offending braggart will usually be a large man with a loud voice telling all and sundry what he has caught, how he

25

caught them, and that everyone else was doing it wrong. He will be standing, legs splayed, arms folded, next to the counter, for maximum exposure. This information can still be useful but has to be graded and sifted more carefully, because it comes with more . . . er . . . lumps.

This is why tackle shops with gleaming new rods and reels, racks of tackle and the aroma of maggots can never, and should never, be replaced by internet shopping. Information, and in particular local knowledge, is a massive part of angling, and you can't find those nuggets on a computer, because if you can Google it, so can thousands of others. So support your local tackle shop. If you go in there you might even get a free cup of tea, hopefully minus maggots.

Armed with hemp, luncheon meat, a newly acquired bait dropper and a spot of newly digested knowledge, I headed one afternoon to the River Kennet. It felt good to be driving west. I get the same feeling when I'm driving home after a day in London – I start to relax. As much as I enjoyed fishing my local river, the Colne, it is an urban river for the most part, and you are never far away from noisy cars and aircraft noise. Driving further west towards the quaint town of Aldermaston, the city's sprawl began to fall away. I turned off the M4 at Reading and began to see signs for Woolhampton, Thatcham, Brimpton, all names I associated with barbel fishing lore.

The river was located down a small lane next to the Post Office in Aldermaston. After parking up, careful not to block the farmer's gate, I walked across the field anticipating my first glimpse of the river. It didn't disappoint; clear, gravel-bottomed runs could be seen between beds of bright-green ranunculus weed swaying to and fro in the powerful current. It screamed barbel! Resisting the urge to start fishing straight away I decided to walk the stretch. I think we all have a kind of sixth sense to some extent, and some swims on a river or lake will stand out and beg to be fished more than others. It pays to follow your instincts. Having walked the bank, I decided to dropper some hemp in a swim I really fancied, and fish it just as the light was fading. Meanwhile, I would spend a couple of hours in a nice-looking slack upstream, though I thought of that first swim as my 'banker'. I wasn't really feeling it in the slack area, so it was with great expectation I moved downstream and settled in to my pre-baited spot at around 9pm.

It had been a hot day but now the sun was beginning to set and calm descended on the Kennet Valley. I was using my trusty John Wilson quiver-tip rod and 5lb line straight through to a size 8 barbless hook and a big piece of luncheon meat. This was held on the gravel bottom with a 4 swanshot link leger. Keeping it simple. The atmosphere was electric as I sat there, my concentration on the quiver tip, nodding occasionally with the pulse of the river. This is my favourite part of the experience, the delicious anticipation of just knowing you are going to catch. But one hour turned into two, full darkness came and my rod tip was now illuminated by a torchlight. Maybe this barbel fishing lark wasn't so easy. Still no hint of a bite. Another angler appeared behind me, and he looked like he knew what he was doing.

Clutching an armful of rods and peering out from underneath the brim of his standard issue floppy specimen hunter's hat, he told me that the river had been fishing quite hard lately. He was a barbel fisherman, and said he'd had some good ones from the stretch earlier in the season. After a brief chat, he headed upstream. *At least I'm in the right place,* I thought, and concentrated on the rod more intently. It was deathly quiet, save for the hooting of an owl in the copse of trees opposite. And then it happened.

The quiver tip made a peculiar rustling motion, and then the rod disappeared suddenly from the torchlight as something grabbed the bait and, with great speed and force, headed downstream. No need to strike: the fish was on! The power of the fish surprised me and my adrenalin flowed as we struggled in the darkness. I was in no doubt that I was attached to a barbel. A chub would have thrown in the towel by now, but this fish had other ideas. The rod bucked and pulsed as the barbel hugged the streambed using its flat underside and powerful pectoral fins. Eventually the fish tired and I was able to scoop it up in my landing net. I left it to rest in the river margin while I sorted out my scales and camera. To be honest, I was in need of a rest myself. I'd never caught anything that put up such a fight and I began to understand why the barbel has garnered such respect from anglers. What's not to admire about fighting spirit and sheer strength and power?

Lifting the fish onto the bank, I felt the tinge of guilt that I experience to some extent whenever I catch something. That

moment ended, however, when I saw just what an amazing creature it was. In my mind, a barbel was black and white, like it was
in the photo taken by the Avon all those years ago. Now, on the
soft grass lay a fish with burnished bronze flanks, vivid vermil-
lion fins, a unique underslung mouth and those characteristic
barbules. Very impressive. I cradled the fish for the obligatory
photo, which gave the whole thing a kind of symmetry, but this
shot was me as a man, 26 years on, and in colour.

CHAPTER FOUR

Battling With The Beast

It was an autumn afternoon in 1980 as I made my way along Clapton High Road. I was heading back home after a day in London's West End hawking demos of some new songs I had written. I was down on my luck at this point. Urchin, the band I'd pinned my hopes on, and had spent the past five years nurturing, was floundering. Co-guitarist Andy Barnett had left the group and the punk movement of the previous few years had forced the more traditional rock bands, like us, to the sidelines. True, the so-called New Wave of Heavy Metal was gaining momentum, but Urchin was never going to be a metal band. We were doing goodtime bluesy rock, and as good as I thought we were, it looked like we were going to fall between the cracks.

The day I'd spent up west hadn't gone all that well, and I was dragging my feet as I crossed Lea Bridge roundabout and headed towards Upper Clapton. I was flat broke, which is why I was walking and not riding the bus. Looking up, I saw two familiar figures making their way towards me. It was Maiden's Dave Murray and Steve Harris. We stopped for a chat. They said they had just returned from a European tour with US mega rockers KISS – and their debut album was riding high in the charts. They certainly looked prosperous, with new leather jackets, smart jeans and boots, and very long hair.

'How's it going with you?' they inquired.

I told them that Urchin was inactive for the moment and had a moan about punk rock, all the while tugging self-consciously at my own locks which I had cut to medium length the week before. I noticed as I was talking that Steve was looking at me very intently, and even Mr Murray's trademark grin had been replaced with an expression bordering on seriousness. This probably stemmed from the fact that the pair had rung me several months before to ask me to join Maiden. I had, after working my way through a half-pack of cigarettes and countless cups of tea, called them back to decline their offer. Urchin was still going strong at that point, I explained, and I was happy singing, playing and writing our own stuff.

There was a momentary gap in the conversation and the three of us stood there on the pavement, a stone's throw away from where Dave and I had grown up and taken our first faltering steps on the rock 'n' roll ladder – our heads full of dreams about being in a successful band one day. Steve broke the silence.

'We might be needing a guitarist,' he paused, 'If we call again, will you do it?'

The tone in his voice was clear. This was no polite enquiry on his part. More like, *this is your last chance.*

I got the message.

'Yes, definitely. I think it would be great!' I said.

We bade each other goodbye – Dave now with a reassuring grin and Steve giving me one last look. I continued on my way, head spinning. The call came some time later and the rest is history, well, music history anyway. What if I hadn't bumped into them that day? What if I'd taken the bus instead? Or maybe meeting them had actually provided a subconscious nudge that convinced them to give me one more try.

Another chance meeting, though not quite as life changing, put me on the trail of my biggest barbel. It was the evening of the second day of a 72-hour session in pursuit of the *Tinca tinca.* The trip was hard and ultimately biteless despite fish fizzing all over the swim. The angler wandered into my peg and we started chatting. The conversation led to the discussion of another of the club's waters, a stretch of the River Thames near Windsor. He said it was a good bet for barbel. I remarked to him that I'd already had a walk along the stretch but didn't really fancy it due to there being almost no flow.

'Oh, they are there,' he assured me and told me two anglers had caught over 40 barbel between them over the course of three nights 'bivvied-up' on the bank. 'Fish the middle,' he told me. 'There's more current than you think.'

Now, I would have taken all this with a pinch of groundbait, but the fact that he also mentioned he was a relative of the great angler and Drennan Cup winner Len Arbery told me his words warranted some further investigation.

The summer drifted into early autumn, and I still hadn't managed to catch a tench from this particular lake, despite seeing some huge fish skulking under the canopy of trees and bushes that line the bankside.

It's about this time of year that I start to think about river fishing, specifically for chub and barbel. I knew, and had fished, all my local stretches of the River Colne and over the years had landed quite a few 'doubles', culminating in a personal best of 13lb 6oz from one of the stretches controlled by the Uxbridge Rovers Angling Society. I had, however, never really got to grips with the Colne's big brother, the Thames. At that point a plan began to form in my mind: what if I approached it in the same way as the River Ebro in Spain? On the Ebro, the going tactic for carp was to mass bait, using large halibut pellets. Keep the bait going in and the fish would turn up. If the barbel were in the Thames stretch in numbers, I didn't see why the approach wouldn't work there too.

Large buckets of pellets were purchased along with some 24ml Mainline crab boilies. For the best part of two weeks I visited the river on alternate days, baiting up, but not fishing. The swim in question featured a pleasant, low, grassy bank, with a large bush overhanging the water upstream to my left. The water was very shallow close in, shelving off sharply about 15 yards out. The shelf was bordered by a row of cabbages. Downstream, another large bush jutted out over the margins. Unfortunately neither bush was deep enough underneath to place a bait. Despite looking tempting, the water there was only 18 inches deep.

So, the main baiting was aimed at the middle of the river in around 9 to 12 feet of water. Sometimes, I would bring my collapsible 'portaboat', which just about squeezed in my car, as this fishery had the added bonus of being able to park behind your swim.

On these boating trips, I'd make up grapefruit-sized balls of fishmeal groundbait, which I would lob over the side having rowed out to midriver. This, reminiscent of a scene from an old British war film, with depth-charges fired off the stern of a destroyer, and huge plumes of water rising as the sea-bombs were unleashed. Instead of high explosives, these depth-charges carried pellets and boilies, as well as hemp and maize and a large stone in the middle to sink it. A slightly less combustible mix, but one I hoped would ignite this particular swim.

All this took place during the week, and I had only seen a few other anglers. These were carpers mainly, who seemed to favour the downstream end of the fishery well away from me. I had decided I had done enough baiting up and now it was time to get the rods out.

It was a pleasant early autumn afternoon when I set off for the 20-minute drive to the river. On arriving at the fishery, I parked up and walked through the copse of trees to my swim. To my relief I saw no one was fishing there. I'd had visions of turning up and finding an angler ensconced in the swim, slumped in his chair, exhausted from heaving barbel. But no . . . I pretty much had the stretch to myself.

I was in no hurry. It was only early in the evening and I wasn't going to start until an hour before dusk. Full of anticipation and confidence, I assembled my gear. Two 1¾ Wychwood barbel rods were matched with two Shimano 5000 baitrunners. On one rod the 10lb reel line would be attached to a standard bolt rig with 2oz flat lead, and 10lb Gardner coated braid. A 24ml boilie on a short hair combined with a size 10 hook completed the set-up. This would be cast to midriver, right on the pre-baited area. The second rod was rigged up with a running rig and a large halibut pellet. This would be fished a third of the way across, on the edge of the baited area. I'd heard that the stretch had produced some very big chub so, with this in mind, I hoped the running rig would fool a wily old barbel. Rods were placed on buzzers and angled towards the water, hopefully avoiding one of the many boats that passed by. No need for rods pointed to the sky like anti-aircraft guns – Trent style – Old Father Thames was barely awake from his summer lethargy, and the flow was gentle. The afternoon gave way to a typical autumn evening and the sky was bathed in a pink light as a slight mist started to form, creeping over the river. I cast both rods out and adjusted the bobbins, Delkims set low. I planned to fish until around 2am. With this in mind I'd brought some food to cook on the bank. I sat back as the evening darkened, the smell of chicken stew burbling in the pot, radio tuned to the local station, football upcoming. This was a moment of anticipation – with bells on.

I was washing the stew down with a cup of tea and a Kit-Kat, and Arsenal had edged Spurs 1–0, when the near rod buzzer let out a couple of bleeps. *Here we go*, I thought, placing the brew on the grass slowly, eyes glued to the indicator. I lifted into the fish and was met with solid resistance, followed by a heavy kick. Fish on!

After giving a very respectable account of itself, the fish was drawn over the marginal shelf into the torchlight. I netted the fish and brought it to the mat at the back of the swim. It was a bream and a good one, deep bronze and chunky. It was 8lb of river slab.

I returned the bream, re-cast the rod and reset the bobbin. Five minutes later I was in again. This time the resistance was minimal and I basically just wound the fish in. I was surprised then when a big old chub swirled in the light of my torch. On the scales he went: 5lb 8oz. I returned the old-looking fish back to the water, where he possibly thought twice before having a go at any more halibut pellets.

Half an hour passed when the far rod absolutely ripped off. Barbel! No doubt. Solid resistance and a pulsing sensation down the line as he hugged the river's bed. After a short battle, I landed the fish. At 6lb, he wasn't a monster, but he was my first Thames barbel. This pre-baiting lark was working out pretty well. Yes, I had stacked the odds in my favour a bit, but I had spent the last month blanking on the tench pit . . . swings and roundabouts.

This first session pretty much set the tone for the next six weeks or so. Fishing from dusk into the wee hours, I would catch bream or chub (I caught the old fella again!) at first, then as the night progressed, the barbel would come on. I even managed a double-figure barbel at 10lb 6oz. At the end of every session more boilies and pellets were fired out to keep the fish in the area.

One session turned out a little differently. It was getting well into November now and the nights were getting cold. The party boats that rode the river carrying young revellers were begin-ning to thin out – just as well as I was getting a bit fed up with hearing 'I Will Survive' and 'Dancing Queen'. Maybe the chub and bream were getting cheesed off with Abba as well because on this particular night there was no bream or chub activity and I only managed one bite.

It was the usual barbel 'screamer' and we battled to and fro for a good while. On previous nights I had been wading out across the shallow river margin to net the fish but now I realised

I'd forgotten my wellies. I was debating whether to go in anyway when the still-unseen fish dived into a snag – the sunken branches of a nearby tree. He who hesitates . . . when I did retrieve my wading boots from the car and went out to the snag, the fish was long gone. It had felt like a good 'un, a new personal best maybe. And by the time I got home I had convinced myself I'd just lost a record barbel. Wild imaginations, us anglers.

I couldn't wait for the next session. I was convinced now that all the baiting up must surely be drawing some special fish into the area. I reached the river as usual, a couple of hours before dusk, and settled into my normal spot. I decided to dispense with the niceties and go for broke. Both rods were baited with two 24ml crab boilies and set up with bolt rigs, small PVA bags of broken boilies and pellets were attached, glugged with a foul-smelling crab attractant. I cast both rods to midriver and sat back to await events.

I didn't have to wait long. It was barely dark when the left-hand rod slammed round and the Delkim screamed. I grabbed the rod and wound down. The butt creaked as the blank was wrenched over and the fish charged angrily downstream. A good one. The fish then settled down and headed slowly upstream, pulsing heavily. I carefully donned my waders, all the time keeping close contact with the fish. I waded out to the edge of the drop-off and battled the fish from there. Up and down he went, steadily mostly, then all of a sudden surging off with almost irresistible power, causing me to crouch down and cram on the pressure. Finally the fish was ready for the net. With the barbel safely ensconced, I sloshed my way back to the bank, gasping slightly and headtorch awry. I left the fish in the water, in a carp-style net, while I set up camera and scales.

When all was ready and I had recovered my composure slightly, I retrieved the netted fish and laid it on the mat. When I peeled back the net to have a look at the fish, I gasped. It was massive! The first thing that struck me was the depth of the fish, almost carp-like in its bulk. It was also in pristine, scale-perfect condition. What a prize! The scales read 15lb 8oz, and a new personal best. I was elated. I fished on but no more fish came along so I packed up and headed home.

The stretch of the Thames in question produced a 17lb barbel for a lucky angler the following season. Unfortunately, word spread of this fish and the section became busy over the next few years. I didn't get to fish there for another two years and it was October 2016 before I set foot on its banks again. There seemed to be a lot more anglers but I decided to use the same tactics as before. I baited the same spot heavily for a good week before wetting a line. Despite putting in half a dozen sessions, I never had a bite.

CHAPTER FIVE

A Very Big Chub

'Chub,' said Uncle Stan. 'Two of 'em, under that tree on the far bank'.

It was around the late 1960s and we were on the banks of the Millstream, an offshoot of the River Lea around Stanstead St Margarets in Hertfordshire. I'd never even seen a real chub, let alone caught one. I'd looked at the odd grainy picture in the

Angling Times, and of course in Bernard Venables's *Mr Crabtree Goes Fishing* comic-strip books. I read Venables's stories over and over. The chub he portrayed was wily, strong, aggressive and sometimes even predatory. In Venables's evocative illustrations, Mr Crabtree and his 'apprentice' Peter are crouched on the banks of an idyllic stream, concealed behind various bits of foliage. Mr Crabtree whispers, 'Don't alarm the chub Peter or we won't get another chance soon!' Peter, wide-eyed, swings out his freelined lump of cheese across the river to an eddy, a textbook chub lie. The next drawing is still vivid in my mind. It is of a big chub, in the foreground, and having now engulfed the bait it dives wildly for the bankside tree roots, looking angry and defiant, as you would. In the background is the caption, 'Strike Peter!' The rod is bent double and the line cuts through the water.

'I can't hold him!' gasps Peter.

'Keep the pressure on, he'll yield soon!' says the pipe-smoking, trilby-wearing Crabtree. Exciting stuff.

The Millstream was a favourite destination for me and my dad's Sunday outings. On quite a few occasions we would be accompanied by Dad's mate Stan, or Uncle Stan, as I called him. Stan was what you might call a 'character' and quite a bit older than Dad. They had met early one Sunday morning on the platform of Clapton railway station, both being laden with fishing tackle. They struck up a conversation and then a friendship. This was further strengthened when my dad got a car. Stan owned the local tackle shop right next to the station. Before you get the idea Stan was some kind of business mogul, think again. The shop was tiny. Think Ronnie Barker's *Open All Hours* set in a broom closet. It had a tiny shop window and, on yellowed pegboard, a few rods hung along with assorted Intrepid reels. And flies. Not beautifully tied Palmers or mayflies, but dead bluebottles mainly. Lots of them. This was due to the maggots Stan kept behind the tiny counter. The smell of ammonia inside the shop, especially in the summer, was staggering. This was further enhanced by the fact that Stan also had a sink at the back and was partial to having a wee in it. He delighted in telling a story of how he was caught 'midstream' when an elderly lady came in for some seed for her budgie. He managed to complete the 'task in hand' and also serve his customer at the same time.

Years later, in my early teens when I thought fishing no longer 'cool', I would pass his shop on the way to Dave Murray's house. Now, instead of a fishing rod I would be carrying a guitar, and platform shoes had replaced wellies. I'd meet Stan as he scurried to the betting shop a few doors down, or stood, with bald pate and brown shop coat, in the doorway of his shop. He would look me up and down as I approached, a stub of roll-up perched beneath his grey, Victorian-era moustache.

'All right, boy?' he would say as I tottered past.

Ahh, today's youth, he probably thought.

Having Stan along for our Sunday fishing jaunts was never dull. He was a mine of fishing stories, though early morning car rides could be quite hazardous. The expression 'wherever ye be let your wind go free' gives an indication of what I mean. Mid-anecdote he would pause, tilt slightly, and let forth an enormous fart. 'Sorry, Fred, it just slipped out,' followed by his high-pitched laugh.

Stan was a good angler and he usually managed to winkle out a specimen tench or bream whenever we went out. Good angling on those low-stocked waters of my youth.

My first brush with a decent-sized chub was on the River Lea at Wormley. Dad and I had driven up early one summer's morning. The venue was noted for its tench. We had fished through the early morning without much success and now, around lunchtime, I wound in and went for a look around.

I crossed the humpback bridge to the other side and walked up towards the famous Kings Weir fishery. Here the canalised Lea spills into a larger pool and the stream follows the course of the original river. I looked down onto the weir imagining huge chub and barbel finning beneath its turbulent waters. I pressed on, the bank becoming more overgrown. I eventually came to another, much smaller weir. It was probably no bigger than a tennis court, overhung by trees and full of interesting currents. The air was cooler here and the atmosphere slightly charged. Maybe the noise of the rushing water coming over the sill from the canal above made me slightly more alert. Someone or something could creep up behind you unheard above the hissing of the weir. It also screamed chub and I hurried back to fetch some tackle.

My 12-year-old imagination in overdrive, I returned to the weir pool armed with my Apollo Taperflash rod and some lobworms. I'd pinched a largish hook from my dad's tackle box but now, as I prepared to tie it on, I saw it was a spade-end type. I had been shown how to tie these a few times but had gotten used to using the recently introduced ready-made hook to nylon. Impatient to get fishing, I hurriedly tied the hook on and cast my big worm anchored by another 'half-inched' swanshot into the middle of the swirling pool. The bait came to rest just on the edge of the current and I placed the rod, tip upwards, in the rest. I crouched, eyes glued to the rod tip as it pulsed with the current. Suddenly there was a tap-tap on the rod tip and then a violent wrench. I grabbed the rod, heart racing. I was attached to my first chub. The battle was thrilling but short-lived and I was soon drawing the fish towards my landing net. I could see the hook lodged in the big white lips and the bronze flanks of the fish as it came towards me, inches away. Then it was gone . . . I stared at the line fluttering in the breeze. The sound of the rushing water increasing in volume as my heart slowed and reality flooded back.

It's funny that my youthful fishing memories are full of lost fish as much as fish landed. That chub was probably only a pound and a half, but the weight of disappointment was considerably more. When I inspected my line I could see that my hastily tied knot had come undone. Patience has never been one of my strong points and here it had cost me my first chub. But you learn from your mistakes, so they say.

In the following years I did manage to catch a few small chub. But probably owing to the rivers Dad took me to, my personal best stood at a mere pound or so. Having drifted away from fishing in my mid-teens, it wasn't until the 1990s that I tried fishing for chub again. I had parted company with Iron Maiden by then. The eighties had been something of a whirlwind of touring, travelling and recording, almost non-stop. While I'm grateful that I had the chance to do it all, it did consume me for the better part of ten years. The rock 'n' roll lifestyle is hard to resist, especially when almost everybody else around you is living it. Work hard, play hard is the motto. Drugs, mainly cocaine, were freely available – no need to buy it as other musos, crew and fans were always offering it around. Booze was on the dressing-room rider and in those days we would always have vodka and brandy along with cases of beer. A little 'thirsty' when you're in your hotel room? No problem: minibar. Tour bus? Always well-stocked. While I've never been on stage and performed drunk or high, for most of the time between 1980 and 1983 I was probably very hungover on stage.

The second half of the 1980s saw more of a responsible attitude on my part. We were starting to do big headline shows worldwide by then and you had to be able to do a high-energy show six nights a week, while travelling overnight to the next city by tour bus. While we could get away with playing a 40-minute support set on a few hours' sleep and a banging headache, it wasn't so easy with a headlining show. That's not to say I lived like a monk, and ten months on the road were still littered with plenty of heavy nights. I also suffered with depression from time to time, and drink and drugs only served to aggravate the symptoms. I was quite shy by nature so drinking was an obvious crutch. Sometimes I wish someone had put an arm around my shoulder and got me some help. Instead, everyone just used to laugh at my pissed-up, coked-out antics. People were too busy surviving the crazy life on the road to worry too long about someone else – unless you weren't doing your job, of course. I saw plenty of good musicians and crew members fall by the wayside, losing their jobs, wives and sometimes their life. So, in a nutshell, that was my eighties. A decade of incredible highs and some barrel-scraping lows.

I did a lot of fishing in the 1990s. I had bought a house in the famous Colne Valley. I didn't realise it at the time, having spent the last decade hardly ever having any time off in the UK, but it turned out that my new abode was minutes away from such famous carp locations as Savay, Harefield and the Cons, to name but a few. I also had the delightful and underrated (in those days) River Colne on my doorstep. Not being into carp at that stage, I fished this river almost exclusively through the early to mid-1990s, and gradually upped my personal best chub to a very respectable 5lb 5oz.

The mid-nineties saw my move into barbel and then carp fishing. I hadn't fished the Colne for a good few years. By now I had re-joined the band and we were enjoying something of a resurgence. In 2006 we released our fourteenth studio album, *A Matter of Life and Death*, and in October 2006 we set off on tour to support the record, completing 47 shows in 21 countries, including the USA, Canada and Japan.

We did have some breaks, however, and in May 2007 I found myself back in the UK with some time to kill. On an impulse, I decided to have a walk along the Uxbridge Rovers stretch of the Colne. It was a pleasant day and the river was starting to come to life. Streamer weed skimmed over gravel runs, cabbages were pushing their way to the surface and even the odd mayfly could be seen skipping on the water.

'Looks nice, dunnit?'

A voice stirred me from my reverie. He was an older man and an angler. He must have guessed I was an angler, too, probably by the way I studied the water hungrily, like anglers do in the close season. Look but don't touch.

We chatted for a while, then the conversation turned to chub. At this point, he reached into his wallet and produced a photograph of a whopping great 'chevin' – another name for chub – caught from this stretch, he said. Although he hadn't weighed the fish, it was obvious from the photo that it was a real specimen, 6 to 7lb or more . . . If I was pondering getting a ticket for the stretch, I definitely was now.

But first, duty called and I was back on the road for a short run of 12 shows across Europe on the *Matter of the Beast* summer tour. It wasn't until late June that I managed to have my first session on the river. I set off one afternoon for the ten-minute drive to the stretch. Parking in the lane, I carried my stripped-down kit the five-minute walk to the first peg just below a small weir.

I had a rucksack with a few bits and pieces; my trusty John Wilson quiver-tip matched to a 5000 series baitrunner. The reel line was a 10lb Maxima through to a 10lb sink link braided hook length. A little on the heavy side but better safe than sorry, particularly as the stretch held some big barbel too. Hookbait would be a large hair-rigged halibut pellet.

First, I had to prepare several swims as I planned on roving the river. It was my first visit to this particular stretch, and I thought it would be a good way to find out a bit more about the different swims.

I had just bought a large bait dropper and I crammed this with hemp and various pellets, laying down a carpet of bait in several different swims. Unfortunately my new secret weapon proved too much for my old JW rod when I swung the over-loaded dropper a tad too enthusiastically. The blank crumbled just above the ferrule, leaving me without a top joint.

'Well, I never did!' John Wilson himself would have probably said. What I said was a bit more colourful. Luckily I had a spare in the car. Well, I was in the Boy Scouts, for all of half an hour. On the plus side, I thought the time it would take me to grab the replacement would give the three or four swims I'd baited time to 'stew'. I tucked the rest of my gear in some undergrowth and headed back to the car.

I returned a while later and set up in the swim just below a small weir. Here the water raced over the sill, down over gravel shallows before emptying into a deep far-bank run. It was here

I expected to find fish. I lobbed my tackle out into the flow and put the rod, tip up, into the rest. It was by now about 8pm, but still bright. It was the summer solstice and it didn't get fully dark that day until gone 11pm.

I managed a nice barbel in the first swim – a muscular 8lb fish – but the next two hours produced no bites as I fished my way downstream in each of my pre-baited swims. Finally I came to the last spot. It was a comfortable peg with a small platform perched low to the water on scaffolding poles. The water itself was about four feet deep, with a hard gravel bottom and a canopy of trees overhanging the river for 20 yards or so downstream. It was now nearly dark as I swung my bait downstream towards midriver. Having forgotten the torch I usually use to illuminate the rod tip, I removed my headtorch and then spent a minute messing around positioning it on the platform, facing up and pointing to the rod tip. No sooner had I returned my attention to the rod when it slammed round, disappearing from the beam of light.

I grabbed the rod and the clutch on the reel whined as the fish took the line. The fight was brutal. *Typical barbel*, I thought. It was a good five minutes until the fish was ready for the net. By this time, I'd managed to grab my headtorch and put it on. Up to now, the whole battle had taken place in the dark. I could hardly believe it when, in the light of the torch, I drew an enormous chub over the net cord.

I weighed the fish straight away. The needle on my scales said 8lb. While I rested the fish in the net, I thought for a second that I might have landed a new record. Unsure, I phoned a friend. He didn't know exactly either, but thought the British record stood over 9lb. No record then, but an exceptional fish all the same. I was in a bit of a daze and I gave myself a few minutes to calm down. After readying the camera for some self-take shots, I went to retrieve the fish from where it had been resting in the margins.

Looking down in the landing net, I was gobsmacked. The fish was a colossus, a freak of nature. I lifted it out and gently transferred it to the weigh sling for another look. This time the needle showed just under 8lb so I settled on a weight of 7lb 14oz. I took some pictures, then released the fish back into the river, admiring it again for a few moments before doing so.

I found out later that this was a known fish in the stretch and almost certainly the same one that I saw in the gentleman's photo back in May.

Meanwhile, back in the 1960s on the banks of the Millstream, a young boy strained his neck to see above the stinging nettles and get a glimpse of two big chub under the far-bank willow.

'You going to 'ave a go, Stan?' said my dad to his mate. Stan paused for a moment, eyes squinting as he watched the two chub, face wreathed in tobacco smoke.

'Nah,' he said. 'Too crafty those buggers. Anyway, the pub's open.'

Stan, as usual, had the last word.

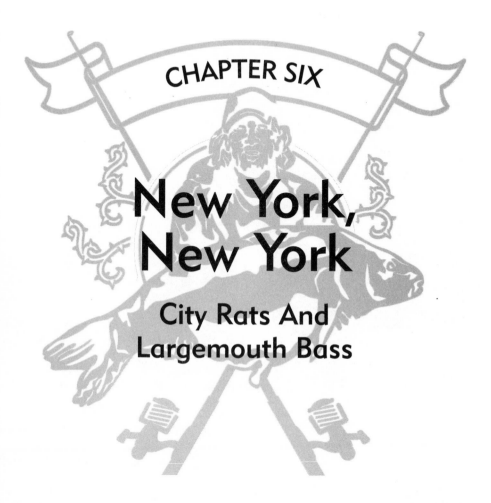

CHAPTER SIX

New York, New York

City Rats And Largemouth Bass

I first visited New York in the summer of 1981 during Maiden's *Killers* tour. I remember arriving late in the evening having driven down from Albany in upstate New York. On that first US tour we were travelling in two hired station-wagons, the gear going in a 3-tonner with our skeleton road crew. The drive down from Albany had been quite pleasant. Clive Burr, Dave

Murray and I were together in one vehicle, the smokers' car. As was the norm, we had crashed out on the first part of the journey, propped up on pillows 'borrowed' from the previous night's hotel. We awoke, compared hangovers, then chatted, excited to see this city we'd heard so much about.

Darkness had descended as we reached the outskirts of Manhattan. Deserted streets were flanked by grimy warehouse-type buildings. Steam poured from manhole covers, rising up from the sewers beneath. A burned-out car smouldered under a neon streetlight. A typical New York scene. The only thing missing was a trilby-hatted mobster lighting up in a doorway. Our excited babble had given way to a heavy silence, until Clive broke the ice. ' 'Kin' hell mate, don't stop, whatever you do!'

We drove on, our spirits rising as the streets grew more crowded, the lights brighter. Eventually we arrived at our home for the next five nights, the Gramercy Park Hotel. The Gramercy nowadays is an artsy five-star 'destination' hotel. Back then, although favoured by the Stones, Andy Warhol and the like, it was a bit of a dump. Unusually, we were all assigned our own rooms. I had, up to this point in the tour, been sharing a room with drummer Clive Burr. To say that Clive lived life to the full would be an understatement, and tales of rooming with him would warrant a book on their own. Suffice to say, I was glad of some space, and a 'suite' no less.

The suite, I had been informed, had just been vacated by actor/pugilist Mickey Rourke, who had rented it on a long-term basis. By the look of it, Mickey had suffered a few rough nights there (he and Clive would have been great roommates). The room was dingy and cluttered with old wall-mounted photos and knick-knacks. It seemed totally suited to a nocturnal life-style. Heavy curtains blocked any unwanted natural light, and in the gloom you could almost see visions of debauchery past, a ghoulish Keith Richards slumped in a corner . . .

I don't remember much after that. I do know that we played four shows opening for Judas Priest at the Palladium (or the Quaaludium as it was affectionately known). Some people thrive on the energy – or neuroses – of NYC. I just remember a sense of oppression and it's a feeling that remains to this day to some degree. I just don't like New York. I have learned to get along with her, though. I'm a bit of a foodie so these days I enjoy trying new restaurants there, and I have one or two friends who I can hook up with for tennis. Fishing, though never far from my thoughts, is not at the forefront when in NYC.

Fast-forwarding to 2019, this time was different. I did what I always do before a US tour: scan the internet for an alternative to staying in Manhattan. The result is always the same. No matter how much I look, I'm always shoehorned back into the city as everyone assumes that you want to be in the thick of it. Statue of Liberty? No! Times Square? Save me! But base yourself outside the city and you are condemned to hours and hours of commuting to and from shows in heavy traffic and, as David Letterman says, 'In New York City, traffic lights are just a guide-line.' So, if you can't beat 'em . . .

This time we would at least have a room with a view, 20 floors up in a swanky hotel on South Central overlooking the park. Having some greenery to look at makes all the difference, and gazing out over Central Park I thought I saw a glimpse of water through the trees. There are several fishable lakes in the park, including the Central Park Lake and the Pond. The former I knew was also a boating lake so I crossed this off my fishing hitlist. Harlem Meer in the north of the park is also fishable but with the mere mention of the word 'Harlem' conjuring up probably very outdated visions of gang war and murder in the back of my US-seventies-cop-show-fed mind, I decided to give that a miss also. The Pond it would be then. The good news was that it was only a five-minute walk away.

We were due to play two shows in Brooklyn on the *Legacy of the Beast* tour. Today, though, was a day off and, after having slept late, it was around 6.30pm before I grabbed my little three-piece travel rod, pocketed a few lures and headed for the Pond. Once out on the street I was immediately swept along in a current of humanity. I certainly didn't stand out trudging along the busy sidewalk with my now fully made-up rod. A man passed me wearing a standard-issue pimp uniform; full-length fur coat, feathered hat, the works. This in 90-degree heat and humidity. A bit further along, a stunningly beautiful model posed amid the throng, elegant and poised as her little photographer scurried around looking for angles.

I was glad for the relative peace and quiet of the Park, although it was hardly an idyllic fishing haven. Dog walkers, cyclists, skateboarders were everywhere, as couples canoodled on lawns and park benches. At least there were no cars. The Pond was actually a pretty good size and looked to extend to around three acres or so. Scanning the murky water for signs of life, I noticed large patches of bubbles as fish rooted around on the lake's silty bottom. I knew the ponds in the Park held carp, some of them very big, as my mate Spug had caught one there a few years previously. These were not my quarry, however, as hooking and playing a carp in such surroundings would attract too much attention and drama. No, today's target would be that most American of fish, the largemouth bass.

The bass is the most popular of American sports fish and, like the carp in the UK and Europe, is at the centre of a multimillion-pound industry. Big-dollar tournaments feature regularly on television. Professional bass anglers, logoed up from head to toe and equipped with high-powered multicoloured fishing boats, compete for prizes that can sometimes be in the hundreds of thousands of dollars. Camera crews follow the leading anglers. When a fish is hooked, it is literally wound straight in and dragged aboard the boat, with no playing or apparent enjoyment on the fisherman's part. All business. The weigh-in takes place usually in a setting not unlike a rock show or political rally. Cheering crowds, sometimes in the thousands, cheer wildly as 'Billy Bob' or whoever raises his catch above his head, like a warrior of old holding aloft the severed head of an enemy. There are tears and hugs. The fish are returned alive, though, probably none the worse for their 15 minutes of fame.

You could be forgiven for thinking this is all a bit distasteful and about as far away from an angling ideal as you could get, that the fishing industry in an effort to 'sex up' fishing has lost touch with the essence of the sport. But, for all this razzamatazz, the anglers involved do possess amazing skills and knowledge. The waters are usually massive, and the pockets of fish relatively small, hence the powerful boats. Lure fishing is all about covering the water. Yes, they have fish finders – sonar devices that can detect fish underwater – but having tried using them myself a few times I can say that mastering them is a whole different skill on its own. The pro-anglers have an arsenal of rods onboard, each of these pre-rigged with different lures. Fish may be feeding at any level in the water column and each lure has a specialised purpose. Surface poppers, diving plugs, rubber 'creature' baits, weedless set-ups designed to skip over submerged structures such as logs . . . all these must be tried in the quest to work out a feeding pattern on the day.

But, back in Central Park, rather than competing against other anglers, I would only have to deal with the crowds, and the abundance of turtles that made a beeline for me every time I approached the shore. Normally, disturbance would be the kiss of death when you are fishing but experience has taught me the fish get used to it over time. This reminded me of when I was on an earlier American tour. We were staying at a hotel in Milwaukee very near to a marina connected to Lake Michigan. I went for a walk in the morning, pausing to look over the bridge that spanned the canal connecting the marina to the main lake. The water was very coloured and, in between the numerous boats that passed to and fro, I noticed the odd patch of bubbles fizzing up here and there, often a sign that there are fish feeding. I nipped back to my room and grabbed my fishing gear. I had a 12-foot telescopic 2½lb TC Carp rod and reel, plus a few odds and ends of terminal tackle. I also had a little Fox Micron buzzer but no bank stick or pod. Bait would be some sweetcorn purloined from the hotel kitchen.

I made my way back to the bridge and then down a stair-way that led to the marina itself. There was a wooden gangway that went along the side of the boat landings and several floating docks. I chose one of these docks, thinking it would be an ideal spot. I even managed to screw my bite alarm in the gap in the wooden slats from which the dock was made. I set up a simple running leger rig with three grains of corn mounted straight on the hook. Moored at the adjacent dock was a 'party boat'. These are basically just a large square pontoon, fitted with chairs and tables and enclosed at its edges by railings, probably to stop its drunken patrons falling overboard. With a large outboard at one end, the occupants can cruise around and, well, party.

This one was thankfully empty and, if there were any carp about, I thought a bait placed close under the hull would be a good bet. I swung the rig out and it landed with a plop, inches from the pontoon. I placed the rod on the little Micron and flicked on the baitrunner. A few grains of corn were under-armed next to the boat and I settled down to wait. It was a

Saturday and as the summer's afternoon wore on, so the canal became busier. Huge cruisers and absurdly powerful-looking speedboats went by in an endless procession out to the main lake. Then the inevitable happened. A party of revellers made their way along the gangway and boarded the pontoon. *There goes the neighbourhood*, I thought. There were three couples, and they dragged an enormous cooler aboard. Soon the party was gaining momentum, drink flowing and rap music blasting from the onboard stereo. And the worst thing was, these partiers weren't going anywhere. You can guess what happened next. I caught two high double-figure commons that afternoon, from under the pontoon, with the party in full swing a few feet above the feeding carp.

Consequently, the noise in Central Park wasn't a deterrent. In the first spot I tried, I managed to climb the small fence that surrounded the lake and make my way to a relatively secluded fishy-looking bay. Casting skill is very important when lure fishing. If you can propel your lure under tree canopies or tight into a bankside structure you will catch more bass. Watching a good lure angler at work, you almost get the feeling of impatience, the angler constantly moving, covering water.

My first cast went sailing straight into a far-bank tree. After a bit of tugging and shaking of said tree, the lure – a rubber crayfish – fell and plopped appetisingly into the water below. I tightened up and began a slow, jerky retrieve. Bang! Fish on! But, as quickly as it smashed the lure, it was gone. A bass, most likely. Encouraged, I fished on in another spot. I watched a raccoon foraging on the far bank, just a few feet from New Yorkers out for an evening stroll. A bit further on I met two young American anglers. We chatted for a while and one of the guys informed me that he'd caught bass up to 5lb from this pond. I told him about the raccoon I'd seen.

'Oh yeah,' he said, 'They're nasty. They will fuck you up!'

Suitably warned, I pressed on.

It was getting dark now and I came to a concrete culvert. Here rubbish had accumulated, blown by the afternoon breeze. Plastic water bottles and Coke cans bobbed on the surface. Standing on the culvert I cast across the small bay to where a group of teenage girls were giggling and screeching atop a large bankside rock. Before I had a chance to wind up the slack, I noticed the line snaking across the water as a bass made off with the rubber lure. I wound down and set the hook. The rod bent sharply as the bass jumped a foot clear of the water, landing with a resounding 'smack'. A minute later, I landed a genuine NYC largemouth bass. It was a well-conditioned fish of a couple of pounds or so. Looking at the raised spiky dorsal fin, the jet-black eyes and the disproportionately large mouth, it was an image of belligerence: 'Eh! Watchoo' lookin' at?'

I returned the fish to his home and he shot away wildly, scattering a school of small bluegills as he did so. Maybe he was a New York cabbie in another life . . .

It was fully dark now and I was glad I had brought my torch, but switching on the light revealed a scene straight out of a Hammer Horror film. Rats. Loads of them. Everywhere. Big ones, small ones, scurrying seemingly unnoticed in the main by the patrons of the still-busy park. I'm used to seeing the odd rat while out fishing but this was on a whole different level. I abandoned my plans to fish into dark and beat a hasty retreat back to the hotel.

CHAPTER SEVEN

Miami

Peacock Bass
In The City Of Vice

Although I was looking forward to the next tour, I wasn't really looking forward to going to Miami. But with the second leg of the 2019 *Legacy of the Beast* tour coming up and Fort Lauderdale the first gig, 'The City of Vice' was the logical place to rehearse. Yes, it was a wrench to leave the UK and its tranquil summer lakes and rivers, especially as I'd only spent about six weeks at home that year. I'd be spending three weeks at the Ritz Carlton in Bal Harbour, North Miami. Yeah, I know, sounds good and 'ritzy'. Literally. What's not to like?

Well, Miami, a bit like Vegas, is all down to how you see it. Go there with a vacation attitude and you'll probably have a lot of fun. You can marvel at the multimillion-dollar yachts, roar around on those jet skis all day, then eat and drink yourself into a coma of an evening. Not bad . . . but I had come to work and my mind was on the upcoming tour. And I don't like jet skis.

This was to be my seventeenth US tour with Maiden. For our first, the *Killers* tour in 1981, we were the lowly opening act playing a 30-minute set for Humble Pie and headliners Judas Priest. I had joined Maiden in October 1980. Now here I was, almost four decades later, gearing up for another run.

On the drive from the airport to the hotel, I looked out and surveyed the scene. Twenty-foot-high billboards stood out against the neon skyline. 'End Erectile Dysfunction Now. RING 1 800 UPPP.' 'Angry Lawyers 4 You!' Endless shopping malls. In America you can buy almost anything, immediately, in sharp contrast to the UK where a request for even the most run-of-the-mill item will result in a sharp intake of breath followed by a 'I haven't got any of those in stock at the moment . . . it'll take a couple of weeks . . . or so.' That's one of the good things about touring the USA: it's so user-friendly, nothing is too much trouble.

A build-up to a tour will see me pause for reflection, like a boxer before a fight. Insecurities nag the mind. Have I prepared enough? Shit, I know I should have practised more instead of buggering off fishing! Unlike a fighter, though, there is unlikely to be physical pain and punishment, just a deep-down nagging fear of blowing it in front of 15,000 fans. Like a dream when you find yourself walking down a crowded high street clad only in a string vest. So, fear is a great motivator, and I need a bit of it to keep me on my toes.

I'd brought my fishing gear, of course, as there are opportunities aplenty to wet a line in the USA. I had packed a separate case with tackle, some bass fishing kit, mostly plastic worms, drop-shot rigs, etc. Also, I had purchased a couple of telescopic carp rods, so they went in my heavy-duty rod holder along with a brolly, bank sticks and landing net. Buzzers and terminal tackle were stashed in among shoes, socks and stage clothes. Bait choice was simple. American carp are not as discerning as their UK counterparts, so corn or tinned chickpeas would suffice. The gear would be stowed away on one of the tour trucks until needed.

I'd arrived at the hotel the previous night and, tired after the long flight, went straight to bed. As usual when travelling east to west, I was up early the next day, bright-eyed and hungry. After ordering eggs, bacon and coffee on room service ($90.00: 'Thank you very much, have a great day, sir!') I thumbed idly through the hotel magazine. There wasn't much content, just adverts trying to sell you stuff you don't really need. 'Your car defines you' proclaimed one such ad. Really? Unfortunately that sums up the Miami 'Strip' where show overshadows substance. The thin end of the American Dream maybe. A lot of the Miami population come up from tough places where material wealth is hard to come by, thus, when obtained it has to be displayed big, loud and proud. But like the music that blares out of every neon-lit club (masquerading as R&B but in reality little more than computerised slush) it is a bit soulless.

I was reminded of one of my long-term fantasies, pulling up in front of a fancy, pretentious hotel or nightclub, in among Ferraris and Porsches, in a rusty old banger. I would lurch to a stop and exit the vehicle, the engine still running, clanking and banging, smoke belching from the exhaust pipe which is dragging along the ground. Straight-faced I would demand the valet park my car and please mind the paintwork . . .

I drew back the curtains and from my balcony on the fourteenth floor I had to admit the view was impressive. To my right was the Atlantic Ocean and directly in front a channel connecting the sea to the maze of canals and lakes that stretch away to the west and ultimately the Everglades. I was reminded that the good news was that Florida is considered an angling paradise. The Florida Keys boast some of the best flats fishing around, with snook, tarpon and record-nudging bonefish all within a two-hour drive from Miami. Inland you have Lake Okeechobee, one of America's largest lakes and one of its most prolific largemouth bass fisheries, and Miami itself is criss-crossed with canals all holding fish; carp, tilapia and all manner of exotic species thrive here, including peacock bass.

Peacocks were introduced 20-odd years ago. Native to the rivers of the Amazon Basin, these voracious predators were brought in to control the invasive species of fish that had made their way into the Miami waterways. Except for periods of unusually cold weather when some died off, the peacock bass thrived, though they didn't grow as big as their counterparts in South America. In the Amazon, a 20lb fish might be average whereas the biggest ever caught in Florida was around 12lb.

I had some experience of targeting peacocks. A few years before we had been in Miami rehearsing and I had booked a guided trip to go after them. Covering lots of water with a boat and with the help of an expert pro, I caught quite a few of these fish. I enjoyed the trip. The fish were a good average size, hard-fighting and strikingly beautiful, a bit like our British perch but more vivid. A lure presented anywhere near a fish produced an almost psychotic reaction that day, with the bait disappearing in a vortex and the rod bucking violently in the hands.

This time, I decided I was going to go it alone. No guide to tell me what bait to use, where to cast, and so on. I saw this as more of a challenge. After some research, I had shortlisted three or four locations that I would try.

First, though, was the small matter of tour rehearsals. We were due to start that very day, so early afternoon saw me heading down to SIR Studios in Miami. After saying hello to everyone and swapping a few 'war stories' we ran through the set. As is most often the way, after all the worrying and soul-searching, we tore through all the songs without a hitch. Well, almost. We all hit one or two bum notes, which were all greeted with big grins. Of course, had it been the last run-through, scowls would have replaced the smiles. But as this was 'first day back at school' everyone was pretty happy. It was great to be back with all the band and crew again and know that we still sounded pretty good.

I was free by 5pm. My first thought was, as always, *Can I get some fishing in?* But remembering that I was supposed to be a professional musician, I decided to go back to the hotel and get some guitar practise in, hit the gym and get an early night. I pretty much followed this routine all week up until Thursday. We decided to take a long weekend to give Bruce Dickinson's voice a bit of a rest. Now was the time to break out the rods.

First on my list was a section of canal near the Falls mall about 15 minutes south of Miami. After practising in the morning I headed off in my rented Toyota around mid-afternoon. On arriving at the Falls, I parked up and went for a quick look at the canal, which ran through some manicured grasslands between the mall and a pleasant suburban neighbourhood. It was quite narrow, about 20 yards across, and featureless save for two bridges, which were about half a mile apart. These would be the places I would target first. I walked back to the mall in search of a bite to eat.

After a lunch of delicious chicken empanadas (basically pasties) I grabbed a rod and some lures and headed for the canal. As I approached the first bridge, out of the corner of my eye I saw something the size of a small cat move. An iguana. Then another. Loads of them! They scattered at my approach, some slithering down the bank, others diving full length with a splash into the canal. This was another non-native species that had settled in Florida. I was beginning to see a pattern here.

Undeterred, I flipped a rubber shad imitation weighted with a large shot into the shaded area under the bridge. I let the bait sink to the bottom, then twitched it slowly back towards me. Nothing happened until I was just about to lift the lure out to re-cast when ... bang! Something seized the lure right under my feet. My first thought was that one of the iguanas might have grabbed it, but I needn't have worried as one minute later I landed a largemouth bass of about a pound.

This is going to be easy, I thought. The fish had other ideas, though, and the next hour passed with no action. Moving up to the next bridge, the same pattern followed. First cast under the bridge, and I felt a 'plink' on the line, then a slow draw. A moment later, I swung another largemouth ashore, a carbon copy of the first. I fished on into dusk with no more action, and made my way back to the car. Walking along the canal, I was tired and my cotton shirt was soaked through from the heat and humidity. As I trudged through the gathering darkness, my mind turned to critters or, more specifically, alligators. The Everglades are full of them, of course, but they also often make their way into cities, usually by canal ...

I thought back to an experience many years ago. Again we were rehearsing in Florida, this time for the World Slavery Tour, in support of our *Powerslave* album, of 1984–5. We had set up camp in Fort Lauderdale but, far from the five-star luxury we enjoy today, were staying in a rundown motel. To give you an example, one day I decided to rearrange the furniture in my room. Now when I say 'rearrange' I don't mean a TV-out-the-window-bed-in-a-swimming-pool Keith Moon romp. No, this was simple feng shui. On rolling the couch away from the wall I recoiled in horror as what seemed like a hundred cockroaches scampered for cover. It still makes me shiver to think of it.

One Saturday while staying there, Dave Murray and I decided to rent a car and go and check out the Everglades. We were told that there was a dock where you could rent a boat, buy bait and tackle, and even have lunch. Very civilised. After a short drive we arrived at said dock and parked up. The place was quite busy, with boats coming and going. Fishing in the USA can be quite different to the UK. Whole families will go out for a day on the water and anything caught will go into the pot at the end for a family fish-fry. Nothing wrong with that.

Dave and I decided against getting a boat and opted to just fish off the dock itself. I was just remarking to Dave that all the logs floating about must be a bit hazardous for the boaters when one of the 'logs' came swimming towards us. Alligator! It was huge. It swam slowly towards where we were standing and stopped about 20 yards out, facing us, its great, scaly head half out of the water and its soulless, reptilian eyes unblinking. It was eyeing us up as a prospective meal. One wrong move, boys . . .

The Everglades are also home to a particularly venomous type of snake known as the water moccasin or cottonmouth, and its bite can sometimes be fatal. As the name implies, these snakes like to live on or near the water. There is also a number of exotic non-native species including pythons, which can grow to 12 foot. As I was walking along the canal back towards the Falls mall, I could just imagine the headlines. 'Rock star swallowed by python! "Fans saddened but tour must go on," says band. "It's terrible, but we don't want to make a meal of it . . ." '

I'd had a few bad experiences with snakes in the past. Once, my wife Nathalie and I were fishing up near Reading, Northern California. We had found a nice little lodge that had a lake with some good trout fishing nearby. When I asked the owner if there was a boat I could use, he said there was. It hadn't been used for a while but it should be OK. He told me where to find it and off we went to the lake.

It was just a fibreglass rowing boat, stashed by the lake's shore in some bushes, upside down. The oars had been placed inside. We righted the vessel, gave it a quick clean-up to remove some debris, and dragged it the short distance to the water. Soon we were drifting along, Nathalie calmly reading a book and me thrashing around with my fly rod. After a little while, she got fed up of dodging my wayward casts and asked if I could drop her at a small jetty nearby. I rowed back, dropped her off and began to make my way back out into the lake. When I was about a hundred yards from the shore, I noticed a movement towards the back of the boat. I watched in horror as the head of a snake appeared. It was looking directly at me, the rest of its body uncoiling from underneath the wooden seat in the stern. We stared each other down. I didn't know what kind of snake it was but I did know there were a few nasty ones in California. So I started to row back to shore, cautiously at first, then picking up speed, my eyes never leaving those of the snake. Nathalie, noticing that I was heading back prematurely shouted out, 'What's up?'

'There's a bloody snake in the boat!' I shouted through clenched teeth, though it probably sounded more like 'Thsersh sha gloody shnake in da goat!'

I made it to shore, coming in at speed and beaching the boat, then, leaping backwards out of the boat, landed on my backside before scrambling away.

Nathalie had caught the whole thing on her little camcorder. On the film, you can clearly hear her laughing in the background.

Back on the canal, I was glad I had remembered my head-torch. I quickened my pace and was glad to make it back to the air-conditioned safety of my car.

Over the next couple of weeks I tried two or three more locations in search of my first 'self-guided' peacock bass, but failed to land one. Some of the areas I fished were in, shall we say, less salubrious parts of town and I must admit to feeling a tad uncomfortable on some occasions. Miami has an above-average crime rate, so I thought it might be a good idea to find some other spots to try. Enter Filipe, the concierge at the hotel. He saw me in the lobby one night with my fishing rod and asked me how I'd done. It turned out he was a keen angler and very know-ledgeable concerning local hotspots. He recommended a place called Greynolds Park. The canal there held peacocks, he said, and it was only a ten-minute drive from the hotel.

Greynolds Park was an interesting proposition. The main part of the park was set beside a large lagoon. At one end was a massive set of sluice gates which led into a short section of canal followed by another set of floodgates into the main waterway. One side of this was saltwater and the other brackish water, Filipe had told me, though I couldn't remember which was which. Since peacocks don't do well in the salt, I needed to find out. I decided to try the lagoon side first. I tied on a rubber shad and powered a cast upstream, towards the sluice. The water was deep and turbulent as the sluice was partially open due to recent rainfall. It was one of those spots where you would expect a wrenching take immediately, but nothing happened. I was just about to lift the lure from the water for a re-cast when something shot out, missile-like, from the depths and smashed into the shad. Barracuda! As suddenly as it appeared, it was gone, its razor-sharp teeth severing the line, taking hook, lure and sinker. At least now I knew which side was saltwater.

I was just about to make my way to the other side of the sluice when another monster appeared. A ghostly white shape emerged just beneath the surface in the middle of the pool, then made its way slowly towards where I stood. It was a manatee. I watched, fascinated, as it paused under an overhanging tree to my left. It was a huge animal, around eight feet long. There are lots of them in the Miami area but they are shy and gentle creatures so I felt very lucky to see one so close. I watched the manatee for a while until she'd had enough of my intrusion and drifted slowly off. Sailors of old used to call them 'Women of the

Sea' or mermaids. Maybe it was the rum, or maybe it was those long lonely voyages. I just hoped it was a good omen for me on the peacock bass front.

Now I made my way to the middle pond, casting every eight steps or so. I covered the water down to the second set of floodgates in 15 minutes, but no takes were forthcoming, though I did see a tarpon roll in there. I was making my way towards the freshwater canal along a flat grassy bank when for some reason I felt I was being watched. Turning towards a stand of live oak trees to my right, I saw a crouching figure in the shade. A homeless woman, her possessions scattered around her in a series of tatty plastic bags, the inevitable shopping trolley parked nearby, eyed me, feral but toothless, as I walked awkwardly by. God knows what her story was, probably a life blighted by drugs, booze and mental illness. I had money in my pocket. Maybe I should have stopped and given her some, but I just kept going, feeling uncomfortable. I just wanted to get out of there. Maybe giving money would have seemed futile. She might even have been offended.

I pressed on. Now the temperature was in the 30s with super-high humidity and I was again wreathed in sweat. Peering over the road bridge, I spotted a good fish lurking by one of the large concrete supports: peacock bass! I clambered over a wall and scrambled down by the side of the bridge so I could get a cast at the fish. As I did so, there was a commotion under the bridge and a man appeared.

He was dressed in regulation Florida garb: baseball cap, T-shirt, shorts. Behind him, under the low bridge, I could see a suitcase, folded clothes, a fishing rod. He bade me a cheery hello but there was no threat, no story of a broken life in his eyes. He appeared outwardly normal except he was living under a concrete bridge, in 95-degree heat, surrounded by iguanas, snakes and God knows what. This was a recurring theme in my fishing adventures around Miami. Homeless people seemed to be everywhere, perhaps attracted by the warm climate. I decided to give him the little privacy he had, and move on.

The stretch of canal beyond the bridge looked good, wide, with lush grassy banks. It could have been an English Fenland river except for the palm trees that lined the adjoining road. I made my way along the bank. I decided that instead of making random casts I'd wait until I spotted a peacock in the clear water. I soon had my chance. About halfway along the stretch I came to a small weed bed next to a drainage pipe and here, close in, I could see two peacocks. I flipped the rubber shad just beyond the fish, let it sink, then twitched it back towards them. The larger of the two fish turned immediately, fins bristling. It didn't lunge straightaway but when the lure was in front of it, pounced. I struck, nothing! I re-cast. Same thing. Again and again. I tried putting a 'stinger' hook towards the back of the lure as the fish seemed intent on only nipping the tail. Still nothing. I eventually tied on the smallest hook I had, then cut the lure down to about two inches in length. Next cast, bang, fish on!

After a short scrap I had my first self-guided peacock bass on the bank. At about 2lb it wasn't huge but what it lacked in size it made up for in looks. An olive-green body, jet-black bars and vivid orange fins. I slipped him back and he shot off to join his mate. It was obvious to me now that the fish were in spawning mode, the response to my lure being out of nest protection rather than hunger.

At that point, I decided to call it a day, the temptation of a cold beer back at the hotel too much to resist. Crossing the road bridge on the way back to the car park, I took a $50 bill from my pocket, put it in a discarded Styrofoam cup and placed it at the foot of the bridge. After the enjoyment I'd had from the canal, I thought it was the least I could do.

Twenty-four hours later, I was standing side-stage at the BB&T Arena, guitar in hand, waiting to go on. No going back now, no room for self-doubt. The intro music finished and we ran on and launched into an uber-fast version of 'Aces High'. Lights, crowd, action! The gig went well, very well in fact, exceeding our expectations. Then again, with it being the first show on the tour, we didn't have high expectations.

Back at the hotel, I sat back, glass of wine in hand, and studied the tour itinerary, or 'The Book of Lies' as our tour manager referred to it. I hadn't really studied it up until then for fear of feeling overwhelmed. Now, with a successful show under the belt, I looked forward. Let's see, Hartford, Connecticut . . . big carp in the Connecticut river . . . Montreal, smallmouth bass in the St Lawrence . . . Winnipeg, always fancied having a go for those big catfish in the Red river . . . and so on. The endless road and winding river . . .

CHAPTER EIGHT

A Canadian Adventure

Trout And Bears

The aptly named World Slavery Tour was 12 months of virtually non-stop touring in 23 countries. When we finished the tour in 1985, I went back to LA and checked into the Oakwood Apartments. So-called burnouts take many forms. For some rock stars who have just done too much of everything it's a sort of blaze-of-glory scenario. It usually starts with a drink-and-drug binge and an ill-advised 100mph car ride. Said rocker is then pulled over in his red Porsche. The car is full of drugs, hookers, guns. The star doesn't go quietly. He struggles and is pinned to the ground. By this time, the vultures are hovering: the media flies above the unfortunate star, beaming live pictures onto our TV screens.

The mighty have fallen, but wait . . . six months later, our rock star has done rehab, is born again, and is an anti-drug crusader. He has donated some (probably a minute amount) of the profits from his new album to charity. The album is a smash and the media is full of his tanned, clear-eyed and (new) white-toothed mug. This is usually an American scenario. British rockers are a bit more low-key and us lot will usually sport a 'stiff upper lip'. Brit musicians will usually manage to drag themselves onstage no matter what shenanigans have happened the previous night (or nights). As Keith Richards said, 'Rehab is for people who can't handle their drugs.'

Having said that, we're all of us human and while it's hard for the average person to sympathise with a burned-out rock star, there are pressures from the lifestyle and issues unique to perform-ing. Sometimes you walk the high-wire of success and are not always able to deal with it. People pay their money for a show and expect you to be 'on' every night. Of course, this is impossible, and when you are young and inexperienced, putting on a bad performance (in your own mind) can seem like the end of the world. The doubts can start creeping in. 'I'm shite, I'm a fraud. I should never have done this.' Perfectly normal responses but, as a young person, it's all too easy to have a drink to soften the edges, then another and maybe a line, and another . . . seeking oblivion, a refuge from yourself sometimes. Then, feeling like shit, you repeat the whole process again until it becomes a habit.

I certainly suffered from this from time to time, and as I sat in a gloomy apartment in LA the walls started closing in. There was, however, sun just behind the clouds. The phone rang – that old-fashioned ring like on *Columbo* or *Hawaii Five-0*. It was Nathalie. I had met her at Dave Murray's wedding in Hawaii and I had come back to LA, hoping to spend some time with her. Not only did I find her attractive but I was intrigued because she had told me she won first place in the State Jackpot fishing tournament off the island of Maui, Hawaii. I suggested that she come over and I'd cook her dinner. To this day, I don't know why I said that. I was certainly no cook. I just blurted it out. She agreed and I dashed out to do some shopping.

We dined lavishly that night on fish fingers, chips and peas. Talk about no idea . . . at least I had bought some decent wine.

Dinner over, we sat on the sofa to finish our wine. Being an experienced seducer of young ladies, I reached over and grabbed the TV remote control. She must have inwardly groaned.

I flicked through the channels and stopped on something that caught my attention. It was an angling programme. Two fly fishermen were standing knee-deep in a pristine, wide, fast-flowing river. The rocky banks were lined with towering pine trees. They 'whooped and hollered' as one guy brought a large trout thrashing to the net. He held the fish for the camera.

'This is a wild brown trout from Canada's best trout river, the Bow in Alberta. Whoo!' Another rebel yell.

'I'd love to do that,' I sighed.

'Why don't we?' said Nat.

And so it was I found myself on a plane from LAX bound for Calgary. Nathalie had spent some time in Banff, Alberta, and assured me it was just what I needed to decompress from the tour. We landed and grabbed our luggage and went to rent a car. Half an hour later we were on the road to Banff in a shiny black Camaro.

It was dark when we arrived at the Banff Springs Hotel. We were shown to our room up on the top floor of this ornate olde-worlde inn. I tipped the bellhop and he disappeared, then I noticed the bed. At least ten feet wide, it had a huge pink embroi-dered satin heart above the headboard. The honeymoon suite. I began to perspire slightly. Nathalie and I didn't know each other that well . . . I felt really uncomfortable at first but tension eased a bit over the next few days and we started to have a laugh about it. I still hid in the bathroom, slightly embarrassed whenever any staff such as housekeeping came in.

The next morning, I rose early. The hotel is set on the banks of the famous Bow river and I was anxious to explore. I drew back the curtains and was greeted with an almost impossibly beautiful vista. It was mid-July and against the backdrop of the Rocky Mountains, smoky-blue in the morning light, the river tumbled over the Bow Falls. Foaming white water crashed onto the rocks below, before broadening out downstream in a vivid blue ribbon. Stunning. Pine forest lined banks flanked by more mountain ranges for miles down the valley of the river as it flowed on its way to Calgary.

I couldn't wait to get out and fish. Surely a river this beautiful had to be full of monsters? I didn't fly fish at that point. Instead, I carried a 12 foot telescopic rod I had picked up in Spain earlier on the tour. This and a few other bits – reel, some floats and so on – were all I had. I'd come to Canada on a whim and I was seriously under-equipped.

After a bit of breakfast, I grabbed my meagre kit and made my way to the river. It certainly looked the part. Deep and fast-flowing beneath the falls, it featured all manner of fishy-looking spots. The bank was lined with huge car-sized boulders and I spent the morning rock hopping and fishing in the slack water created by the boulders. I'd managed to collect a few worms in the grounds of the hotel but, despite fishing all morning, I managed only one tiny trout for my efforts. This was to set the tone for the first week or so of our trip. Although probably the most scenic place I've ever fished, it was probably the least productive.

That's not to say we didn't have a lot of fun. We loved the hotel and most evenings after a great meal in one of the restaurants there we would head into the quaint ski town of Banff. Our favourite haunt became the Cascade Inn, a rock bar that had live music and stayed open late. We had some great nights in there and got to know some of the locals and even some of the bands that passed through.

I was getting a little desperate on the fishing front, though. One evening, while I was talking to one of the waiters at the hotel, he told me about a lake that held some very rare golden trout. Taylor Lake, he said, was about a 90-minute hike from the nearest parking area, just out of town. It was beautiful and full of trout, he told me. We decided to give it a try and the next day saw us making our way up the pretty trail that led up to the lake. We were running a little late, the result of beer and sambuca chasers at the Cascade Inn. But even though it was getting on for 3pm we thought we could be there and back before dark. Up and up we went, and after two hours with no sign of the lake we realised we might have gone off the trail a bit. Or a lot.

Somehow, by luck more than judgement, we eventually found the trail again and after about five hours we came to the lake. It was certainly beautiful, shallow at one end, then turning a deep emerald green as it got deeper towards the far bank. I had by this time bought myself a little 5-weight set-up and I managed a few clumsy casts into the promise-filled water. Nathalie, ever the pragmatist, pointed out that the light was going and we'd better think about making our way back. Now, I could see the odd trout cruising off the shore. Just one more cast!

'There's bears here, y'know,' said Nat, turning her head slowly and surveying the darkening woods. So that was it.

The hike down was a bit quicker, though picking our way down the steep trail on already sore legs was tortuous. Make it back we did, though, holding hands and edging our way along in the dark for the last half-hour or so.

Back at the hotel and now ravenous as well as exhausted we headed to the restaurant. The waiter, a different guy but super-friendly as always, asked how our day had been. As we told him about our hike to Taylor Lake, his eyes widened. 'There's bears there, y'know,' he said. 'There was an attack not long ago . . .'

This was Canada. Of course there were bears everywhere, and we would see a lot before the trip was through, but I now know that, in Alberta, most of bear attacks leading to death or serious injury have happened in the Banff area. Most of those incidents happened because people who should know better wandered into bear country. Thankfully, there we were having dinner instead of, well, being dinner. Nat and I had a giggling fit in the restaurant, the result of wine, fatigue and probably relief.

We made plans to move on the next day. One of the local anglers had told me about a place just north of Kamloops, British Columbia, called Skitchine Lodge. Located on a remote plateau in Bonaparte Provincial Park, the lodge was surrounded by 15 trout-filled lakes for exclusive use of the guests. Access was via a three-hour ride on logging roads or floatplane. I'd contacted Skitchine Lodge owner Bob Hearn and we agreed to meet at Kamloops on Saturday morning. From there we would take the floatplane up to the lodge.

We checked out of the Banff Springs Hotel on a Friday morning. We thought we'd take a leisurely drive to Kamloops, staying in little motels along the way and generally exploring, fishing and enjoying the scenery . . . and what scenery it was. With every mile we drove along the Trans-Canada Highway I felt the madness and pressure of our recent World Slavery Tour fall away more and more. Of course, I had travelled a lot of miles but ironically I hadn't seen a lot or had a chance to fully appreciate or savour all the places I'd been. Put it this way, if you are on the road with Mötley Crüe, Twisted Sister and W.A.S.P., sightseeing is not exactly top of the priority list. After a while, touring becomes about survival. Trying to get enough rest, good food, etc. You become pretty much a night animal, your body clock wired for 9pm and two hours on stage. The rest of the time is geared around that, or it should be. Of course, after a while the lines of reason get a bit hazy. You come off stage adrenalised, then pile on the tour bus for another eight-hour trek through the night to God knows where. A few beers are followed by a few more. This is what all our heroes did, isn't it? *Could you pass me the Jack Daniels please?* You eventually crash out, only to be woken up an hour later by the tour manager to check into the hotel. You stagger off the bus in the early hours of a new day, hair all askew with a bad case of 'bus head', dragging your Halliburton case behind you. You go, zombie-like, to your room where you will crash out until it's time for the soundcheck, then the whole cycle starts again. Among bands at that time (and still today, probably), there was a kind of silly macho pride. *I've been up all night partying but I can still perform.* I suspect it was a similar culture to footballers of the past.

The guys in Twisted Sister were all down-to-earth, straight-up New Yorkers. They opened up for Maiden on part of the tour and were riding high with a couple of big hits of their own. Guitarist Eddie Ojeda and I always got on well. A few years later I bumped into him in New York City and we went for a beer and a catch-up. I didn't get back to my hotel for two days.

Back on the Trans-Canada Highway we had come to a halt. There was a commotion up ahead so we pulled over on to the hard shoulder and got out to have a look. There, just up ahead, was a moose trapped between the road and the high bank behind. An enormous, chocolate-brown coloured beast, it was like a horse with antlers and it was becoming very agitated. Suddenly, the moose charged down the hard shoulder towards us. Retreating behind the car, we watched as the huge animal thundered past before careening up the bank and disappearing into the forest. I was loving Canada!

We eventually reached Kamloops on Friday evening. After checking into a small motel, we grabbed a bite to eat, then got some sleep as we had to be up early to take the floatplane in the morning. Next day, we made our way to the floatplane terminal on the Thompson river where Skitchine Lodge owner Bob Hearn greeted us warmly. We quickly stowed our gear on the plane and made ready to take off for the short flight to Skitchine. We were excited and a little nervous as the plane taxied away from the dock then began to accelerate across the water before slowly lifting from the river and climbing skywards. The noise of the engine was deafening and we felt every bump as the plane soared then levelled out over the forest of Douglas fir.

After 20 minutes or so we began to descend and up ahead a series of lakes could be seen set among the seemingly endless forest. After one last turn, the pilot lined us up for landing and we came in skimming and then settling smoothly on the water, sending out a huge wake as we did so. We taxied over to the home dock, and the engine was silent as we unloaded our gear.

Following Bob, we trooped up the path to the main lodge, set on a slight hill overlooking the 'home' lake. After checking in, Nat and I sat drinking coffee on the veranda overlooking the water. The lake itself extended for about 30 acres. Directly opposite was Skoatl Point, an extinct volcanic core that rose dramatically from the lush forest. We sat drinking our coffee and drinking in the sheer beauty and the silence. If there was a fisherman's paradise, then this just might have been it. A trout-fishing paradise anyway. These were the famed Kamloops trout, known for their fighting qualities and delicious flavour. We were both certainly going to sample both over the next week or two.

After coffee, we were shown to our accommodation, a rustic log cabin set on its own plot on one of the lake's small bays. It had a simple layout; upstairs a large bed accessed by a wooden ladder, and downstairs a living area with a wood-burning stove and a huge window overlooking the lake. A small kitchenette with coffee-maker, fridge, and so on completed the set-up.

Although Skitchine Lodge was remote and the country was wild, we weren't exactly 'roughing' it. We had a great meal at the lodge that night and met the other guests, a retired couple from Calgary. After dinner we retreated to the bar, where owner

Bob settled down with a large whiskey and gave us a lowdown on what to expect, fishing-wise. The conversation moved on to the wildlife and, inevitably, bears.

'Oh, we had a big old grizzly up here last spring,' said Bob. We leaned in closer. 'I was sittin' right here on my own,' he continued. 'Lodge'd just opened after ice-out and we didn't have many guests . . .' We listened enthralled in the firelight. 'All've sudden there was an almighty crash and a huge paw came through the window. Right here!' He pointed to the window on his left without looking. Bob said he wasted no time and climbed to the loft above, pulling the ladder up after him. The grizzly meanwhile had fully dismantled the window and was making for the kitchen. The only two guests were in the dining room, just finishing their desserts, when they heard the disturbance. On hearing Bob's cries of 'Bear! Bear!' they hotfooted it out of the door and ran down to the dock, where, terrified, they jumped in a boat and headed for the middle of the lake. Eventually, hunger satisfied for now, the bear wandered off and Bob descended cautiously back down the ladder to survey the damage.

'Course, we knew he'd be back, eh?' said Bob. 'So we had to get a sharp-shooter up from Kamloops. He tracked the bear and killed it. Weighed close to seven hundred pounds.' You could have heard a pine needle drop. 'So, yeah, we got bears,' he explained. 'But they won't bother you.'

Bothered or not, it certainly spiced up the walk back to our cabin in the moonlight. We stopped occasionally, straining our ears against the eerie silence of the night for the sounds of breaking branches or growls. In the end, we gave up and ran full-pelt the rest of the way, giggling like kids.

The next week was idyllic. Early mornings were spent cradling cups of coffee around the wood stove. After breakfast we could stroll down to the dock, jump into a boat and there we were, fishing for wild trout with a remote lake all to ourselves. The trout weren't big – the largest we caught from the home lake was maybe 1lb – but they were plentiful and rose freely to my muddler minnow.

I was also getting better at casting and, with the help of one of the guides, expanding my knowledge of different kinds of flies. I wasn't that great with boats, though. I think American and Canadian anglers are much more used to boats and motors than us Brits. I always found outboard motors difficult to deal with, seemingly playing up at the worst of times. One morning Nat and I had a little, shall we say, 'tiff'. I can't remember what it was about but it resulted in my going fishing on my own that morning. I told her I'd be back in a couple of hours and strode down the wooden gangway to where the boat was moored. Nat watched me, arms folded, pouting slightly.

There were two other anglers and a guide just getting ready to cast off and I nodded curtly to them as I passed, before jumping in my boat and preparing to launch. With the boat right at the end of the dock and facing inwards towards the lodge itself, I started the engine. Now, I always got a little confused when it came to the throttle and maybe I should have been a bit more careful. Maybe I was still a little wound up about our 'tiff'. In the event, I gunned the motor full ahead instead of reverse. The boat reared like a wild stallion as it tried to mount the dock. At this point I should have cut the engine but in my panicked state I just white-knuckled the thing harder. Screeee! The boat was now almost perpendicular to the dock and the engine, deprived of cooling water, was belching smoke everywhere. Eventually, I came to my senses, cut the throttle and the boat slumped back into the water.

Through the clearing smoke, I could see the other party of fishermen staring, their mouths open in the now-returned silence. With as much dignity as I could muster, I calmly reversed the boat out into the lake and made my way slowly away from the dock.

One day we decided to try one of the outlying lakes. This involved taking a boat across the home lake, then a 20-minute hike through the woods to the other lake. Boats were stashed lakeside there for guests' use. Bob had assured us that this lake held bigger than average trout so I was even keener than usual to get on the water. The day was pleasant, the forest quiet, save for the buzzing of insects. Dappled sunlight penetrated the canopy above. A deep scent of pine permeated the air as we trekked along the narrow trail to the lake.

We found the boat and cast off into the clear water, its edges lined with lily pads. The fishing was very good and after a couple of hours I had caught and released a couple of bruiser rainbows around the 2½lb mark. We were just making our way into one of the small bays on the lake when I spotted a movement on the shore. I paused mid-cast to watch, when a large black bear crashed through the undergrowth over on the lakeshore. It hadn't seen us, thankfully, even though we were only 20 yards away. Safe in our boat, we watched in fascination as the bear went about its business. We could hear it snuffling and snorting as it mooched along the lakeshore, pausing occasionally to raise its head and sniff the air. Then it turned abruptly and crashed back into the forest, its huge rump disappearing into the foliage. Nat and I, silent up to this point, turned to each other mouthing simultaneously, '*That was a bear!*'

We fished on. At this point, I had decided to keep a few trout to take with us. Skitchine had a smokehouse and the result-ing smoked trout it served was delicious. Evening was moving into dusk and I was on about my tenth 'last cast' when Nat (the voice of reason, remember) reminded me we had quite a trek yet to get home. Do you see a pattern here? (I remember my dad getting exasperated with my reluctance to leave the water, though I think he was secretly pleased that I had taken to fishing so keenly.) I finally wound in, then rowed hell for leather back to shore and the trail that led to the home lake. The light was going fast as we started out on the walk. After a while we came to a small clearing and, out of the gloom, a large black shape loomed before us.

'Jesus, it's the bear!' I hissed. We backed off as quietly as we could.

'The fish!' whispered Nat.

'What?'

'The fish! Throw him the fish! That'll keep him occupied and we'll sneak past.'

I remembered the two trout I had kept, lying now in a small landing net I had slung across my shoulder. Terrified, I hurled the fish, net and all, at the bear. Not pausing to look, we circled around. Once we thought we were safe, we chanced a look back.

'He's not moving.'

'It's a tree . . .'

'What?'

We could now see the trunk of a large, fallen tree and at one end its exposed roots and the black earth that clung to them. It looked, taking into account the poor light and the events of the day, like an angry black bear. How was I to know? I'm from Clapton, a bear-free zone. I retrieved the fish, untangling the net from the roots, and we made our way without further mishap to the lodge.

We had planned to stay at Skitchine for a week but we were having such a good time we kept extending. Eventually, after nearly three weeks, we walked down to the dock for the last time and boarded the floatplane for the flight back to Kamloops. As the plane climbed, I reflected on what an amazing experience it had been and just what I needed after 12 months of solid touring with Maiden. The trusty Camaro was waiting, parked up at the airport, and the prospect of hitting the road with no particular place in mind was appealing.

We decided to head north and check out Wells Gray Provincial Park. Before getting on the road we decided to pick up some new music for the journey. We got the eponymous Heart album (the one with all the massive hits) and *Akimbo Alogo*, a record by ex-Max Webster frontman Kim Mitchell and band. The Kim Mitchell album was to become one of my all-time favourites and a big influence. His music became the soundtrack to our trek through Canada (appropriate as he is a Canuck). I spoke to him on the phone a few years later when I was looking for a producer for my ASAP album. But that, as they say, is another story. There was another album I wanted to buy, but had walked out of the record store and had forgotten. The record was by English singer John Waite. Nathalie offered to run back in and pick it up. She came back with the cassette, jumped in the car and we set off on our adventure.

'Put it on then!' I said, as I pulled away. After grappling with the packaging, Nathalie put the tape into the machine and hit play. Now John Waite is very much in the Paul Rodgers bluesy-rock vein, but whatever was coming out of the speakers wasn't that. The car was filled with a baritone growl, like someone waking up in a rubbish skip after a heavy night. Tom Waits! Two more different vocalists you couldn't wish to find. John the archetypal rock frontman, and Tom, well, more grizzled than chiselled.

We spent the best part of a week driving around Wells Gray. Three things stand out in my memory. One afternoon we pulled off the road and made our way down to the river that the road had followed since we had left town. This was Nathalie's suggestion. 'If you keep looking over at the river while you're driving you're going to get us killed!' she scolded. 'Why don't we pull over and you can fish for a while?'

The stream was medium-sized, deep and fast flowing, with a greenish-blue tinge to it. I found a slack area off the main current and set up a long trotting outfit, the rod a 13-foot tele-scopic with a fixed spool reel, straight through to a size 12 hook baited with a big worm. I didn't have much in the way of floats so used one of those crude red and white bobbers you get in general stores over there. I pinched a couple of large shots about a foot from the hook and set up the bobber at about six feet up the line. I stood at the head of the pool and swung the tackle out to the 'crease' where the main current met the slower water of the eddy. Keeping the rod tip high and my middle finger check-ing the line on the open spool of the reel, I worked the bait downstream. The first run through produced nothing, so I set the float up another foot to run deeper. I cast out and repeated the process. This time the bobber disappeared about halfway down the run. I thought I might have caught bottom but I swept the rod back anyway and was surprised to feel the thump of a good fish on the other end.

The clutch whined as the fish plodded out into the main current, the rod pulsing to its every movement. I thought maybe I'd hooked a salmon, but on bringing the fish in I saw it was a dark-coloured rainbow trout of around 2lb. I unhooked the fish carefully, still in the water, then cradled the trout while he regained his strength. I was admiring all the amazing colours on the fish's flanks when Nathalie said bluntly, 'Let's eat it.' We had killed and eaten some fish at Skitchine but they were so plentiful there. I looked down at the trout I held gently in the water, now full of wiry strength and ready to go. 'Maybe the next one,' I said, before the trout shot off into the depths.

Catch and release may be a relatively new concept in places like the US and Canada, but growing up as a coarse fisherman in the UK it was the norm. Most people don't understand the idea of going to all the trouble to catch a fish then throwing it back. I kind of understand that. After all, that was how fishing came about, gathering food, pure and simple. In the hard years of the Second World War, people would fish and keep bream, roach, pike and so on for the pot. As times improved and food became more plentiful, people didn't need to fish for the table as you could just go to the supermarket and buy already cleaned and filleted trout, salmon, cod and so on. Of course, by then angling had evolved. You had everyone from young boys (like me) on places like the semi-polluted River Lea in London snatching bleak and gudgeon to the highly skilled, competitive match fishermen of the Midlands, constantly improving their methods to get the edge over the other anglers. Fly fishing almost became an art form, with fishermen tying and replicating hundreds of different insects from their larval, emerging and finally fully fledged states. Science, etymology, physics, instinct, intuition, perseverance – angling encompasses all these things and that's why I love it.

I think good angling practices are important. Although non-anglers find it hard to understand, any fisherman with a soul will always treat his catch with respect. Of course, anglers fall into different categories and there's unfortunately a minority of people who probably weren't fortunate to have someone show them proper ethics, which, as every good angler knows, are basically these: use tackle that is appropriate for the size and species of the fish you expect to catch; use barbless hooks if possible; don't keep fish out of water longer than you need for a quick snap or preferably not at all; before you actually release the fish, make sure it's regained its strength (this is important for barbel and bream especially in the summer). And pike! They are fragile, despite their ferocious appearance. Hit the run early. If the pike comes off, don't worry, he'll more than likely come back for a second go; if you are going to eat the fish, dispatch it quickly and humanely. Also, don't handle the fish unnecessarily or lay it on rough ground or gravel. Soft grass is OK for medium-sized fish but an unhooking mat is even better.

I certainly wouldn't go fishing if I thought it would cause fish any lasting harm. Panic, yes. Confusion, most likely. Pain? I was always taught that fish couldn't feel pain, but there have been numerous studies over the years and there are arguments both ways. There's no doubt a fish will act a bit pissed off when you hook it, and probably sulks and doesn't feed for a while after capture, but then again, can you compare human feelings to that of a very simple creature like a fish? I think it's up to the individual. Certainly anglers and angling associations do a lot of great work improving fish habitat, monitoring pollution and fish stocking. On most Sundays during fishing's close season you'll see work parties of angling clubs all over the country, clearing bankside litter and desilting streams to improve flow, and they have been doing so for years, quietly, long before environmental issues became 'trendy'.

Back on the river bank, Nathalie was a bit exasperated because I'd let the fish go. I said I'd fish on, and if I caught any more they could go on the grill. After a few more trots down the run, I managed to land a couple of modest-sized trout, enough for lunch anyway. Wrapped in silver paper with a little butter and herbs, they were delicious. We sat on the riverbank eating straight out of the tinfoil with our hands.

At moments like this I'd cast my mind back to the *Powerslave* World Slavery Tour and shake my head at the madness of it all. Back in January 1985 we had been booked to play the first of the now well-established Rock in Rio festivals in Brazil. At that point we had already been on the road non-stop for five months and were due to play a show in Buffalo, New York, before flying down to Rio. We were glad of the thought of a break from the freezing weather of North America. As we watched from our tour-bus windows, snowdrifts seemed to line every road and highway. Life was condensed into show–bus–hotel with as little time as possible in the real world.

The trip to South America certainly started well. As part of our deal with the Rio organisation we were being flown down to the 'Samba City' first-class on VARIG Airlines. We stretched out on the big seats and were served platters of roast beef, steak and chicken, all carved and served by attendants in full waiter attire. This was the life! Rio airport was an early indication of what I know now as the norm for touring in South America. Chaos! Eventually, though, we got our baggage, slogged our way through the traffic and made it to the hotel.

The Copacabana Palace Hotel was like a who's who of rock 'n' roll at this point with various members of Queen, Whitesnake, Ozzy and AC/DC wandering around. I bumped into John Sykes, then Whitesnake guitarist, in the lobby. John's from Blackpool and we'd met when my pre-Maiden band Urchin had played there at a place called Jenks Bar back in the 1970s. We planned to go out for a beer and a catch-up. The problem was, nobody could get out of the hotel. Fans had swarmed into Rio from all over South America and now hundreds were camped outside, waiting for a glimpse of anyone who looked like they were in a band. Even sitting out on your hotel balcony trying to have a quiet breakfast, people would come to their windows in the adjacent apartment blocks, waving, shouting or, worse, just staring.

The gig itself was equally mad. The organisers had built a revolving stage, the theory being that while one band was performing, another could be getting set up, cutting down on the 'changeover' time. Inevitably this went wrong on more than one occasion. I somehow managed to get out front to see Whitesnake (who played just before us). As the stage turned round, stacks of Marshall amps fell like dominoes as leads were caught in various moving parts. Roadies scurried forth, amps were rescued and order restored enough for Whitesnake to take the stage. They were great, too, rising above the chaos to deliver a really professional set.

After watching 'Snake, I made my way backstage to get ready for our performance. As I passed Queen's dressing room, I heard them run through a note-perfect acapella version of 'Bohemian Rhapsody'. Amazing.

The gig was eventful, to say the least. We had no soundcheck, of course, and the sound onstage was awful. We were used to getting by in this situation from our days supporting other bands, our philosophy being to try and ignore any technical problems and just power through it. But this was on another level. All I could hear was the drums, deafeningly loud and distorted. This wasn't Nicko McBrain's fault, of course: it was the monitoring system. Bruce in particular was having a hard time, the vocals on stage being almost non-existent. He played guitar – a Dean model, a sort of Les Paul shape with the trademark Dean pointy headstock – on one song in those days. It was during this song, 'Revelations' that he finally snapped. At the point where the song gets heavy, Bruce went to take off the instrument a bit too energetically and caught himself flush between the eyes with the aforementioned headstock. Blood poured down his face and now he eyed the wedges manically. One by one he booted all the monitors off the stage, sending them tumbling into the pit and causing the cameramen to dive for cover. The whole show was going out on live TV across the country! And the band played on . . . we finished our shortish set and retreated back to our dressing room.

We weren't happy with the show at all and were sitting around feeling miserable. Then Rod Smallwood, our manager, burst in through the door. 'Fuckin' great!' he shouted, beaming from ear to ear. 'The blood, it looked brilliant!' And then we heard it, the crowd were still going mad. That sums up Maiden in those days: you had Queen and Whitesnake up there all polished and slick, then us smashing our gear up and bleeding all over the place, yet still able to win over a new audience.

Of course, back at the hotel that night and the next, the party was in full swing. Everyone was busy having a good time, and not much sleep. Eventually it was time to leave the sun and fun of Rio and continue our North American tour with a couple of dates in New England before a prestigious seven-night stint at the iconic Radio City Music Hall in New York. The fact that we were playing Radio City had raised a lot of interest and the band and fans alike were all looking forward to it. Things were going to take a turn for the worse, though. On the fifth night of our residency, Bruce had struggled through the show with a sore throat. He went straight back to bed after the gig and we all assumed he'd be OK for the show the next night. Meanwhile the rest of us hit the town, and in the early hours of the morning I found myself at the Hard Rock Café with some of the guys from support band Queensryche, feeling slightly worse for wear. I thought it might be a good idea to head back to the hotel and get some rest.

I awoke the next afternoon with a banging headache. I pulled the covers over my head and berated myself for drinking too much the night before. *Oh God, when will I learn? . . . I'll be crap tonight . . . Shit!* My throat was burning as well, on top of the hangover. I knew I was coming down with the 'flu as well. Great. In those days you just kept going if you were ill, and we'd all done shows where we were sick. So I'd be expected to do the same tonight. I hunkered down and decided to get as much rest as possible. Brrrinnnngggg. The phone. Staying under the covers, I snaked one arm towards the bedside table and, after groping around, picked up the receiver. ' 'Ello?' I croaked. It was tour manager Tony Wigens. 'I'm really sorry, Adrian,' said Tone, 'I've got some bad news. We're going to have to cancel the rest of the shows at Radio City. Bruce's really sick, he can't talk, let alone sing.'

'That's a shame,' I said, 'oh well,' and replaced the receiver. I stayed there in bed for the next three days and nights aching, shivering and sometimes delirious. Most of the band went down sick that week. It had all gotten a bit much. We'd gone from freezing our arses off in upstate New York to the tropical sun of Rio, then back to New York, chill factor minus a thousand. No wonder we all got the 'flu.

Of course, we bounced back. Seven days later, we had resumed the tour.

After lunch we headed upstream. Someone had told us there was a waterfall so we packed up our stuff and headed back to the car for the short drive to the falls. After parking up in a layby we hiked the short distance down to the river, following a well-worn trail through the pine forest. The noise was faint at first, becoming louder as we approached the river. We followed the sound of rushing water and eventually reached the end of the trail and the falls themselves. It was quite a sight. The water tumbled over rocks the size of a two-storey house and plunged into a large deep pool below. Then I saw something move in the water. Then again. A fish of about 8 to 10lb leaped completely out of the water. It was bright crimson in colour. Another fish rolled, and then another. They were sockeye salmon and the pool was full of them as they rested there on their spawning run. I watched fascinated for ages before Nathalie managed to prise me away. I can't remember why but I didn't try to fish for those salmon. Maybe I just wanted to leave them in peace. An incredible sight, though, etched in my memory.

Another time on that trip, we were driving up a logging road when it occurred to me that a black Camaro wasn't exactly an ideal vehicle for that kind of terrain. The road itself was mainly loose gravel, and very narrow. It was cut into the side of the mountain and, to our right, fell away steeply, the slope quite bare save for a few spruce trees dotted about. It was late in the day and the setting sun was blazing directly into my eyes. I was trying to get to the river, of course, and although I wasn't exactly speeding, I could have maybe been a little more cautious. Next thing, the outside wheels slipped and we started to slide sideways down the not inconsiderable slope, gathering speed on the loose shale. It was not a nice feeling. Luckily, we only went about 15 feet before some perfectly placed trees broke our fall. Nathalie seemed to find the whole thing hilarious. Myself, less so. Maybe because it was my fault or maybe because I knew there would be no fishing that day. Whichever way, I was mumbling expletives while Nat was belly-laughing, all this taking place while we were climbing through one of the windows, the doors being jammed shut. Amazingly, we were both unscathed and the car wasn't a total wreck. We clambered back up the mountain, slipping and sliding on the loose rocks.

Once back on the road we stood, slightly out of breath, and took stock of the situation. Now what? Just then, a large truck appeared, flashing lights and all. Forest ranger. Great. The vehicle stopped and a large man, wearing an even larger cowboy hat, appeared. He approached.

'How's it going, eh?' he said.

He joined us, hands on hips, looking down at the Camaro. The sleek black speed machine was looking a very sorry sight now, covered in dust and its undercarriage visible, like a horizontal northern lass worse for wear on a night out in Newcastle.

'You from out of town, eh?' he said, still looking down the slope at the car.

'Er, yeah,' I replied, 'London actually.'

'Mm . . . figures,' he said. 'You know that's a ravine? River's down there – it's a two-hundred-foot drop . . . I guess you guys were lucky.'

He made his way back to his vehicle, shaking his head, before calling for the tow-truck. Yes, we had been lucky and, for the first time in a long time, my thoughts turned to home.

It had been an amazing trip and the open spaces of Canada had really helped recharge my batteries. I hadn't been back to the UK in eight months, and I wanted to catch up with friends and family. The next day we loaded up the Camaro and headed for Vancouver where we caught a flight back to LA. From there I jumped on a flight to London. Nathalie would follow in a month or two when I'd sorted out somewhere to live. The band planned to take a break from touring and we wouldn't convene until April 1986 to start work on what would be the *Somewhere in Time* album.

CHAPTER NINE

New Zealand And The Monster Of Rock

It was early one morning in the autumn of 1987. Nathalie was sitting up in bed, thumbing through a brochure. 'Why don't we go to New Zealand? We could get a round-the-world ticket,' she continued. 'It'd be amazing, we could stop in India.'

My future wife's appetite for travelling was still sharp back then. Just as well. I'd just finished nine months on the road touring to support Maiden's *Somewhere in Time*. I sank back under the blanket, all this talk of travel was making me feel suddenly tired.

'They have incredible fishing in New Zealand apparently,' she said, holding out the aforementioned brochure and rattling the pages above my head. I emerged, tortoise-like and blinking, from under the covers.

'Oh yeah?' I said.

The glossy brochure was from a company called Fishing International. They offered angling trips to all sorts of locations; Belize and Panama for bonefish, Mexico for billfish, and New Zealand . . .

'Pristine crystal-clear rivers and streams brimming with large rainbow and brown trout, lakes that hardly see an angler from one year to the next.' I pulled myself up into a sitting position from my previous horizontal. 'New Zealand offers all this and more,' I read on, considerably more awake now; pictures of happy anglers holding enormous trout filled the pages. Maybe the idea of a round-the-world trip wasn't such a bad idea. It would be an adventure, certainly.

In those days, before kids and other responsibilities, Nathalie and I would often undertake spontaneous road trips. I hadn't spent much time at home in the UK from 1980 when I joined the band up until this point. Most of those years were spent either touring or recording, usually abroad. I'd lost touch with a lot of my old friends. I certainly hadn't done much fishing at home since the mid-seventies and was completely out of touch with the UK fishing scene. I was a bit of a vagabond and the flat I was currently renting (from Bruce Dickinson, no less) was the first time I'd had an address in a while.

The *Somewhere in Time* album and tour cycle had been a gruelling yet satisfying experience for me. As with the previous album *Powerslave* the music was written in Jersey, Channel Islands, and recorded at Compass Point, Bahamas. This time, we'd decided to mix the album at Electric Ladyland studios in New York City.

The writing process in Jersey had been a bit on and off. We had taken up residence out of season at La Corbière Hotel in Jersey; the band and crew took over the whole hotel and the gear was set up in the ballroom, the theory being that anytime we were inclined to work on a song, we could all just go down there and play. The reality was quite different. Picture a dozen 20-something guys given the run of a hotel, including the bar, and you'll understand that not a lot of work got done until the last minute. Steve Harris, Maiden's bassist and founder member, would spend a lot of time in his room writing on his own. Bruce, by his own admission a little burned out from the *Powerslave* album and tour, was spending more time fencing with his mate Justin. They would head off to Europe for tournaments. I didn't blame him in some respects. Life on the Channel Islands out of season could be pretty boring. The island, though pretty, had a small-town feel and most of the locals regarded us with suspicion. We were there to write, so I knuckled down and tried to come up with some ideas. I had just purchased a little 4-track cassette recorder for this purpose. Compared to today's technology it was very primitive and not the best quality.

I was sitting in my room one evening messing around with some ideas when there was a knock at the door. It was Steve Harris. He'd heard me working and was curious.

'Well, I've got a few riffs and bits and pieces,' I said.

'Let's 'ave a listen then,' said 'Arry.

I played a few things, with little reaction. I fast-forwarded the tape and pressed play. A descending single-note riff blasted out of my little portable speakers. I immediately pressed the stop button.

'You don't want to hear that, it's not really suitable. It's . . .'

'No! Play it!' said Steve excitedly. I pressed play again. I pretty much had the whole thing demoed.

'I think this'd be really good for the album. Have you got any words?'

I told him I hadn't but that I had some ideas for melodies.

That night after dinner, I went back to my room and finished the song 'Wasted Years'. Funny to think if I hadn't by chance played him the demo, it would never have ended up being a Maiden song. 'Wasted Years' was released as the first single from the *Somewhere in Time* album and we still play it in our live set today.

Back in London, Nathalie and I started planning our round-the-world trip. We bought a plane ticket that would take us to India, Hong Kong, then on to Australia and New Zealand, and finally Tahiti. We touched down in Delhi late one night. India was an eye-opener, to say the least. I was appalled by the poverty and the chaos in the huge city. After a few days in Delhi we had had enough and decided to take a trip up to Kashmir. I had heard there was some good trout fishing in the rivers near Srinagar, close to the border with Pakistan. We left most of our luggage in storage at the hotel in Delhi and took a short flight up north with just a few small bags and a couple of fly rods. Arriving in Srinagar we were immediately besieged by taxi drivers, baggage handlers and beggars swarming all around us. We had booked the best hotel we could find there, a former maharaja's palace. We saw a smiling man holding up a sign with our names so fought our way through the throng towards him. We threw our stuff in the boot, slammed the doors and drew a sigh of relief as we collapsed on the back seat.

'Hotel, please.'

'Yes, sir! You want carpet? My brother has very beautiful carpet!'

'Yes, I'm sure he does. Hotel please.'

'Of course, sir.'

We drove on, bumping over unpaved roads, our driver swerving to avoid packs of dogs.

We came to an abrupt stop a little while later at a large breeze-block building. A goat wandered up and looked glumly through the passenger window.

'Hotel?' I enquired.

'My brother's. You see carpet, then go to hotel, it's on the way,' said our ever-smiling driver. Oh well, when in Rome, or Kashmir, or wherever the hell we were . . .

This kind of set the tone for the rest of the Indian trip, with nothing being as it first appeared. The hotel was a dump, I got the worst food poisoning ever, and the rivers were completely devoid of water, let alone trout, at that time of year. There was also a strong military presence in the area with Kashmir being so close to Afghanistan. The soldiers were formidable-looking characters, tall with hooked noses and blazing eyes.

I also had a bit of trouble on the flight back to Delhi. At airport security I had put my fly rods encased in two metal tubes through the X-ray machine and was waiting for them to come out the other side. I waited, and I waited some more. I tried to ask the guys on the scanner what was happening but they spoke no English. I did get the idea that they wanted me to hurry up and get on the plane, minus my rods. I tried to explain that, at the check-in, I was assured that I could take my rods on the plane with me. They weren't interested and became increasingly more agitated. The raised voices and excitement now caught the attention of a group of heavily armed soldiers. They came over and joined in the fun; cue more shouting and waving . . . Great. They tried to hustle me out, insisting that the plane was about to leave with or without me. I stood my ground and made it clear I wasn't going anywhere without my rods. Meanwhile, Nathalie went ahead to alert the captain of the situation. She later told me she anxiously boarded the plane yelling along the aisles, 'Stop the plane, don't leave without him . . . my boyfriend's fishing rods have gone missing.' The captain and crew looked at her perplexed, and said that they weren't due to take off for another 40 minutes.

Eventually, airport security saw that I wouldn't budge and handed the rods over. I rushed across the tarmac to the waiting plane, escorted by the soldiers. The atmosphere had turned bad very quickly and we were glad when we finally took off and headed back to the relative safety of Delhi.

The next day we boarded a flight to Sydney, Australia, via Hong Kong. From there we would make a 'hop' over to Christchurch, New Zealand. We spent two days in Hong Kong, which I hated. The city was the epitome of hustle and bustle, and you couldn't even go a few yards down the street without someone literally measuring you for a suit. Teenage boys hustled aggressively trying to sell, sell, sell.

I did buy Nathalie an engagement ring, though.

Finally, after a brief stopover in Sydney we touched down in Christchurch. We went straight to the airport hotel, checked in and caught up on some sleep. The journey had been hard and I don't think I've ever been so jetlagged in my life.

Early the next day, bleary-eyed but excited, we loaded up the rental car and headed off to the first fishing destination, Lake Brunner Lodge. Located in Inchbonnie near the west coast, about a three-hour drive from Christchurch, the lodge would be our base for the next week.

The scenery on the drive was stunningly beautiful. We drove along winding mountain roads, stopping now and then to take in a particularly beautiful view. The road followed a ravine, and occasionally the forest would give way, allowing a tantalising glimpse of a rushing, azure river beneath. Finally the terrain levelled out to open farmland and Lake Brunner itself could be seen shimmering in the distance. It was probably the first time the phrase 'achingly beautiful' came to mind.

We arrived at Lake Brunner Lodge in the late afternoon. I was itching to fish at that point and after a quick lunch the lodge manager pointed me in the direction of a spot where I could wet a line for a few hours. I made my way down to Lake Brunner's shore where a river poured its contents into the lake. A more scenic spot an angler couldn't have asked for, and I was full of anticipation as I tied a Woolly Bugger on and unfurled a cast out into the swirling currents. Surely I couldn't fail? I had travelled oceans to get here.

I fished into the twilight, but all was quiet apart from bumping one fish. The thing was, just because I'd travelled miles and paid good money to get to the other side of the world, the trout didn't know that. It reminds me now of when I bought a Gibson Les Paul guitar when I was 18. I was convinced that having saved up to buy the iconic guitar, now I would sound like my heroes. Think again . . . there was a lot of work and pain ahead.

Back at the lodge that evening we were served a delicious meal with local lamb and wine. After dinner we were introduced to our guide for the week, Bruce. Dressed in hiking boots, green shirt, shorts and fly-fishing vest festooned with various nymphs and streamers, he certainly looked the part.

The only thing missing were corks hanging off his cowboy-style hat. We discussed plans for the following day and we decided to fish the local River Arnold.

The Arnold was a medium-sized river that ran out of Lake Brunner and tumbled its way north, 30 miles or so, before meeting the Grey River. The water had a slightly tea-coloured tint and flowed hard through shallow riffles and deep pools. The river held mainly small- to medium-sized brown trout, though there were a few rainbows also. Bruce had picked us up that morning in his truck and, after driving a few miles, we pulled off the road and bumped our way down a dirt track to the river. We parked up in a clearing next to the stream and Bruce got out and surveyed the scene, hands on hips.

'All right, let's get you guys into some treoyt!' he said cheerfully.

'I think he means trout,' I whispered to Nat.

Most of the fishing was going to be done wading, so I had brought a pair of lightweight chest waders and some felt-soled boots to go over them. This might have appeared a trifle soft to a hardened Kiwi angler but, hey, the water was cold. Bruce meanwhile was standing bare-legged and thigh-deep in the rushing river, the water swirling around the bottom of his short-shorts. I approached him in my just-bought shiny new fishing gear: aforementioned boots and waders, new vest and brown cowboy hat. (I wore that cowboy hat comfortably and unselfconsciously throughout my time in New Zealand and Australia. When I returned to London I wore it for about five minutes before I felt like an utter twat.) Bruce turned as I lumbered towards the river.

'Good call with the waders, mate!' he said. 'It's bloody freezing in here!'

I had brought a little 5-weight rod and Bruce advised a Royal Wulff dry fly and a hare's ear nymph dropper. With this set-up you can cover any trout feeding near the bottom on nymphs, the dry fly acting as both an indicator as well as covering surface-feeding trout.

A simple but very effective way to fish these rivers. It's important, though, to fish the nymph at just the right depth so it bumps along the bottom of the stream. In this way it can imitate the natural food the trout are feeding on such as caddis fly nymphs and various insects. Set too deep, and the fly will drag unnaturally and the fish won't take it. Having grown up coarse fishing in England I understood the principle. It was comparable to 'trotting' the stream.

We made our way slowly upriver, casting at any likely looking spots we came to. We caught plenty of trout, too, all browns up to a couple of pounds. The fish came from all sorts of lies, from the obvious 'crease' where fast water meets slow, to rampaging shallow riffles. Although not that experienced at fly fishing, I soon got the hang of it. Many of the same principles apply whether you're after chub and roach in an English river or after trout in far-flung New Zealand. Fish will always look for cover and food supply and, once you have developed your 'watercraft', you will always have a good idea of where the fish might be holding. Having Bruce guiding me didn't hurt either. The guy practically had gills.

I was enjoying myself, trout fishing against a backdrop of palm trees and all sorts of exotic bankside foliage. Nathalie also caught one under Bruce's expert tutelage. Then it began to rain, and rain.

We sat in the lodge staring out at the near-flooded landscape. We'd eventually had to pull off the Arnold when the water levels rose and even the hardy Bruce was struggling to hold his footing in the torrent. Now, it was the second day of the storm but the good news was that it was due to abate that afternoon. The bad news was that the local rivers were unfishable. I was, of course, straining at the leash to fish.

'What about Lake Brunner itself?' I enquired.

Ray Grubb, the owner, explained that they didn't usually take guests there but . . . I think he recognised the symptoms straight away. Trout fever.

'Let me make some calls,' he said.

An hour later, Ray appeared. He had managed to get a boat, he said. Bruce was going to take me out on the lake so I grabbed my gear and we piled into his truck. With boat and trailer attached, we took the ten-minute drive down to Lake Brunner. What followed was one of the most unique afternoon's fishing I have ever had.

We came to a small dock and Bruce and I got the boat in the water and stowed the fishing gear. It had still been raining up to that point but now the rain eased and sunlight split the clouds.

'Ideal,' said Bruce. 'Ever done any bonefishing?'

I had, of course, and most of my limited fly-fishing experience had been with bones.

'We're going to pole the shoreline and sight fish. We should see some cruising trout. Be ready to make a quick cast,' he advised. I stood on the bow, rod in hand, 20 or so yards of line pulled off and resting on the deck, ready to launch. Sure enough, after a few minutes poling along the shore I spotted a trout up ahead, it's back dark against the sandy bottom. 'There's a fish, twenty yards, twelve o'clock!' hissed Bruce crouching down.

'I see it!' I whispered. I waited until the trout was within casting range, then drew back the rod into the one o'clock position. I made a few false casts to judge the distance before plopping the fly about ten feet from the cruising fish. Thinking I was too far from the trout, I readied for another cast but Bruce, anticipating this, said through clenched teeth, 'Leave it!' The trout turned at right angles and made a beeline for my pheasant-tail nymph, and I saw the white of the inside of his mouth as he inhaled the fly. Fish on!

The rod bent and the fish tore off, heading out into the lake, the white fly line bumping and fizzing into the depths. After a few minutes I brought a long, lean brown trout of a couple of pounds to the net. We took a few photos and released the fish, watching it power off back into the clear waters of the lake.

We continued on, stalking trout from the boat and working the shoreline. We caught plenty of fish but I also 'spooked' a few with the odd clumsy cast in the shallow water. After a few hours, Bruce beached the boat and prepared a shore lunch. We sat back and enjoyed smoked trout salad washed down with a local brew. The storm had now fully passed and the mist over the lake had cleared. We sat relaxing on a shingle beach and in the distance the mauve-brown mountains of the Southern Alps rose up into the sky. Tussock and fern lined the far shore, interspersed with stands of a number of exotic trees.

After lunch we set off again, catching the odd fish in what was more like bonefishing than traditional trout fishing. However you looked at it, it was fun, challenging enough to make it interesting but not so hard that it was a grind. We caught no monsters, though. The best brownie pushing 3lb. We pulled off the lake at around 5pm and headed back to the lodge, happy to have salvaged a great day's fishing from an unpromising start. That night, after another spectacular dinner at the lodge, we packed our bags, ready to leave the next morning for the next phase of our adventure: Cedar Lodge, South Island.

Cedar Lodge was located right on the Makarora River near Queenstown. The lodge was unique in that it was one of the first to pioneer 'heli-fishing'. The mountainous region is home to a multitude of streams and rivers, the only problem being access. That's where the helicopter comes in, and every morning groups of anglers are flown off to various locations and picked up at the end of the day. Around the time that we were there, in the mid-1980s, this was the only operation of its kind in the area. This meant different stretches of water could be 'rotated' to greatly reduce fishing pressure. This led to incredible fishing in wild and remote locations.

We drove down to Makarora and arrived at Cedar Lodge in the late afternoon. It was another spectacular drive, incredible scenery, sparkling blue rivers, towering blue-grey mountain ranges interspersed with spreads of open green farmland. We dropped off our bags in the room and went off to do a bit of exploring. When we returned we were invited into the dining room to meet owner and pilot Dick Fraser. Dick was an interesting character. He had hunted and fished in the area for decades and had personally scouted all the locations that the guests fished. He was something of a raconteur also, and he would entertain the guests by recounting some lavish story in the lounge bar at the end of each day. He would always finish with something like, 'G'night folks. See you on the helipad in the morning. I should've sobered up a bit by then,' before disappearing into the night.

He was obviously winding us up, and any doubts about Dick's flying expertise were dispelled the next morning as he lifted the 'copter smoothly off the pad and off towards the mountain range. We were slightly alarmed, though, as he guided us upwards, the blades only yards from the mountainside. Sensing our concern, he turned, smiling, and explained that he needed to be close to catch the thermals to lift us over the summit.

Just as we crested the peak, he turned the machine sharply down the other side, levelling out as we reached the flat country beyond. We settled into a steady chug and I was finally able to release the white-knuckle death grip I had on my rod case.

After only around ten minutes, Dick banked the chopper over a rise and set us down next to our first destination, the Young River. The Young is a small fast-flowing stream that rises in the Mount Aspiring National Park. Don't let the word 'Park' fool you. This country is as wild as it gets and you won't find any comfy benches to sit on, or manicured lawns. We unloaded our gear, ducking under the 'copter blades, before Dick bade fare-well to myself, Nathalie and our guide for the day, Brian. We stood and watched as he disappeared up the river valley, the roar of the blades giving way to the rustling sound of the stream. Brian led the way upriver. The plan was to spot fish, then present them with a dry fly or nymph, depending on the way the trout were behaving.

It was challenging fishing in many ways, not least clamber-ing over the rocks and boulders as we made our way in search of fish. It was tough going but Nat and I did OK, with no dodgy knees or bad backs to impede us back in those days. Then Brian stopped abruptly, crouched and raised a hand. He'd spotted a good fish lying close to the bank just upstream. He motioned me forward and pointed to the spot. Even with Polaroid sunglasses that take the glare off the water, I struggled to see the fish. Brian told me to keep looking, and eventually I could see the faintest outline of a trout, finning behind a medium-sized boulder.

I clambered down the rocky bank and made my way into the river. The rocks in the stream were slippery smooth and I struggled to hold my footing in the heavy current. I got into position about 20 feet downstream of the fish. I couldn't see the trout any more but Brian, higher up on the bank, was directing me. 'Just to the right of that white rock. Put a cast up there,' he hissed, braced against the current. I paid out some line and began to cast. The line flew out and the size 14 Royal Wulff landed with a plop.

'Too short!' whispered Brian. 'You put it right on his tail. Try again.'

I pulled off a yard more line. This time the fly landed perfectly and it had only travelled a foot when it was engulfed and the line drew taut. 'Got 'im!' yelled Brian.

Rod held high, I followed the fish, which had, after a moment of confusion, taken off like a train downstream. After a lively scrap that had me slipping and sliding on the rocks, I netted a good brownie of around 3lb.

That set the pattern for the day: walking, spotting and casting to fish. At around 5pm we made our way towards the rendezvous with the returning chopper. En route there, Brian said he had something to show us. In the miles that we hiked that day, the river had changed character slightly. The brawling freestone stream had broadened and deepened, and the river valley opened out. Brian led us up a bankside bluff and motioned for us to keep low and stay quiet. We crawled to the edge of the bluff and peered over the edge into the deep blue pool below. There, beneath a thick canopy of trees, were around a dozen huge rainbow trout, milling around lazily in the slow water. The smallest Brian estimated at around 8lb. The biggest, easily into double figures. After my initial shock I started to think how I could make a cast to one of those giants. Brian read my thoughts.

'If you can get a cast in here you're a better man than me, mate!' he whispered.

He was right. The wise old trout had chosen their spot well and it was virtually impenetrable due to the thick tangle of branches overhead.

Even an approach from the far bank would have been all but impossible as the canopy almost touched the water out in midstream.

'Don't worry, mate, you'll get your chance at a big 'un,' Brian said as we backed away. He was to be proved right a few days later.

The rest of the week followed the same routine. After a hearty breakfast we would be whisked away in Dick's chopper to some other amazing location to chase trout. Evenings would see us back at the lodge for a great dinner and more tall stories from Dick before discussing the next day's plans with our guide.

One evening we returned to find 'Happy Hour' in full swing. We had fished that day with another guide, Stuart, as Brian had been assigned to look after three newly arrived older American gentlemen and their wives. After landing, I went straight to our room for a quick clean-up while Nathalie went to the lounge to order a couple of cold beers. After around ten minutes I made my way to the lounge, looking forward to my beer. When I entered the room all the guests were present, and all eyes focused on me.

'There he is!' they said as one.

If you've ever encountered older couples on holiday, you'll also know that they can be overpoweringly nice, especially if they happen to be American.

'And he's from England!' they said, beaming.

I froze, a rictus grin on my face. I felt immediately uncomfortable. Despite what most people think, while I like jumping around on stage and genuinely showing off, away from it I'm quite reserved. (Maybe that's why I do what I do.) Now I was the centre of attention in this small room. I glanced over at Nathalie. Her face was a picture: *It's not my fault. You're on your own. Good luck!*

'Brian's been talking about you to us all day,' said one of the blue-rinse ladies, 'Never heard of Iron Maiden myself, but we're real impressed anyhows!' They all concurred and acted, well, impressed. 'And he brought in one of your records!' she said as she lowered her glass of bourbon on to the table (not her first of the evening, I guessed).

Oh God, I thought, *this is getting worse.* I shot a daggered glance towards Brian who was beaming at me. He thought this was a good idea, obviously.

Maybelle — that was her name, honestly — held the album cover up close to her face '*Somewhere in Time*,' she said slowly. 'Gee, look at this, guys! Is that some kind of monster?' she said, her face contorting.

'Er, yeah . . . that's, er, Eddie,' I mumbled.

'Oh . . . it's pretty scary!' she continued

Thank God it's not the Killers *album*, I thought to myself, but the torture was just starting.

'Let's see now . . . oh look, Bob, they have all the words printed out!' she cried.

I didn't like where this was going.

'"Stranger in a Strange Land". Wow! What's that about?' said May.

I told them that I had read the story of the Franklin expedition where the crew had been stranded in the Arctic in 1845. In 1984, the body of one of the sailors, John Torrington, was exhumed, almost perfectly preserved in its permafrost grave. The picture of poor Torrington was published around the world in the mid-eighties and certainly left an impression on me. I was very moved and had based the song's lyrics on this story. Now, it's one thing to hear your lyrics sung by a good singer over a rocking backing track, and another to see them printed off and standing alone on an album cover. Take the music away from Little Richard's 'Tutti Frutti', for example, and the lyrics alone are not exactly poetry. In other words, the delivery is a big part of it.

So, in short, I wasn't looking forward to having Old Maybelle reading out my lyrics, especially as she insisted on pronouncing every word so de-lib-er-ate-ly as people who have imbibed are prone to do. But there was nothing I could do, so I took my beer and tried to make myself as small as possible in the corner.

So Maybelle proceeded to read the lyrics out to her captive audience, holding the album cover close to her face with her right hand. She raised her left occasionally to intensify a particularly dramatic line. When she finished you could have heard a pin drop. Maybelle sniffed and her voice cracked when she said in a quiet voice, 'Well, I'm a little choked . . .'*

It was the second to last day of our Cedar Lodge stay and as usual after breakfast our guide Stuart joined us to discuss plans. Today, he said, we'd be visiting a very special place, the Hunter River. The Hunter was one of the more remote locations that they fished and he told me it had only been visited by anglers once that year. Fishing would be mostly for rainbows with the odd brown thrown in. We grabbed our gear and made our way to the helipad and the ever-grinning Dick Fraser in the 'copter.

After the usual aerobatics, Dick turned the chopper north-west. About 20 minutes later we came to the river valley and Dick set us down and bade us a cheery farewell.

We were travelling light with just a couple of backpacks and a few fly rods. Stuart shouldered the biggest pack and strode off heading downstream. Nat and I looked at each other and rolled our eyes. Stuart, though an excellent technician and very knowledgeable, was a bit, well, grumpy. With long hair, beard and ponytail, this New Zealand back-country man sometimes gave

---

* When Maiden played in Calgary, Canada, on the *Somewhere in Time* tour, we were contacted by one of the team that was involved in the exhumation and autopsy of the three dead sailors. He didn't know much about the band but wanted to make sure that we showed proper respect to John Torrington, John Hartnell and William Braine. He watched the show and we performed 'Stranger in a Strange Land'. Afterwards we chatted and everything was cool. He explained that initially he had thought we were just a bunch of 'out of it' rock 'n' rollers using the idea without much thought. He said that the exhumation had left a lasting impression on the whole team and it was a highly emotional experience for everyone, especially one of the camera team who was a relation of John Torrington and bore a striking facial resemblance to him.

the impression you were somehow infringing on his turf. Maybe he'd guided one too many 'meat hunters' or maybe he'd simply guided one too many altogether. He had taught me a lot over the course of the week, though, and I could now make a decent steeple cast and mend my line to counteract the varying currents much better than before.

Nat and I gathered up our stuff and followed Stu. The going wasn't too hard. The bank was mostly made up of baseball-sized smooth white stones. A few hours passed. To be honest, I don't remember much up to that point. What happened after, though, I'll never forget.

Nathalie had stopped for a rest and I had continued upriver, scanning the water for signs of fish. I came to a section of higher bank and made my way up. It was only a couple of feet but it gave me a good view into the water. To my left, just upstream was a riffle, a shallow section of fast water that tumbled into a deep blue pool directly in front of me. It was like looking into the deep end of a swimming pool. The bottom was made up of the same white stones that were on the bank, so my eyes were drawn to a large dark shape on the bed of the river. It was huge. Surely too big to be a fish? I watched it for several minutes but I couldn't detect any movement. Stuart appeared.

'What d'you think?' I enquired.

'Probably a rock,' he said. 'Then again, I've seen a lot of rocks swim away.'

I decided to run a dry fly over it, just in case. I made a cast up to the head of the pool, flipped a couple of mends – counteracting the drag of the current by moving the line while it was on the water – and the fly drifted perfectly down the middle of the pool. Then Stuart and I gasped as the huge shape rose from the bottom and tilted up under the fly. We could clearly see the markings of a monstrous brown trout, mouth open and gills flaring as he prepared to engulf the fly. I swept the rod back, into . . . thin air!

'Again! Again! Cast again!' said Stuart, his demeanour having changed from dour to now very animated.

I thrashed another cast out, heart pumping and over-excited, the exact opposite of how you're supposed to act to cast effectively. The cast was hopelessly short. I hadn't even loaded the rod in my excitement.

'Slow it down, mate! If you can *hear* your cast, you're trying too hard,' said Stu, having now regained his professional composure.

I took a deep breath and cast again, pausing slightly on the back cast, then shooting the line forward when I felt the rod load up. The fly landed perfectly and began a nice drag-free drift towards the fish, which had taken up station in the same spot. In an almost mirror-image of the first 'take', the fish rose up from the bottom in ten feet of water, tilted its head towards the fly and hung for a second, drifting downstream at an angle while it inspected the fly, and then it took. This time, I waited for a few seconds before striking. The rod hooped over and all hell broke loose as the fish made a crazy run to the far bank. The fight was brutal. Thinking back, I would have been better off using an 8- or 9-weight rod rather than the little 5-weight now bent double in my grip. Eventually I subdued the trout and led it into the shallows where Stuart held the fish – his net was way too small! – one hand around the tail and the other under the belly. It was huge. Thick across the back, deep bodied and long. Stuart didn't carry any scales or a measuring tape but after casting an experienced eye over the fish, estimated it at 10lb easily. It was certainly the biggest fish I'd caught up to that time.

By then, Nathalie had arrived to take some photos as I cradled the fish in the water. After a few pictures I held the fish, head upstream in the strong current. Normally a fish will dart back off to the deep after a few seconds but the big brownie took a full five minutes to regain its strength. Once the fish started kicking against my grip, I let go and the fish waddled slowly but steadily back into the pool. We all stood and silently watched it swim away. I was obviously elated but I also hoped I hadn't over-stressed the fish and that it would be OK.

Fast forward a year. Maiden were playing a gig in New Orleans. The night before the show was free so I was walking down Beale Street, famous for its restaurants, blues clubs and general mayhem. Turning a corner, I bumped into none other than Dick Fraser! After getting over our mutual surprise, we had a little chat, voices raised slightly over a cacophony of blues, jazz and hubbub. The subject of the big trout came up, of course.

'We had another party of anglers up on the Hunter a few weeks after you fished there,' said Dick. 'Stuart was guiding them. They caught a big brown from that pool. He reckons it was the same fish.'

I certainly hoped it was.

The week at Cedar Lodge came to an end and on a Saturday morning we said goodbye to the Frasers & co. We had decided to go back to Christchurch for a few days before heading off in search of more trout in Tasmania. We spent an enjoyable week in Christchurch during which time I locked away the fishing rods. Nathalie wanted to see the famous Milford Sound and so we took a ferry ride there. Another highlight was taking a helicopter trip up to a glacier.

We then flew on to Hobart, Tasmania, rented a car and began the two and a half hour drive to London Lakes. I felt straight away that it had a different atmosphere to New Zealand. Maybe it was the terrain or maybe it was because I was aware of Tasmania's bloody history. White settlers in the 1800s had all but wiped out the native people of the island and even some of its unique wildlife such as the Tasmanian tiger had been hunted to extinction. Where New Zealand had felt pleasantly open and free of crowds, Tasmania's quietness was almost oppressive, like we were being watched by its long-dead inhabitants. Also, we didn't see much water on our journey, the land seeming arid and lifeless. We couldn't have been more wrong, as we were to find out later.

We were glad to reach London Lakes Lodge and a cheery welcome from proprietor Jason Garrett. He showed us the lodge, which was more than comfortable. The tackle room was full of fishing gear, of course; made-up fly rods sat in racks on the wall and nets dried out on hooks. Waders were lined up at one end of the room; above them there was a shelf on which sat a tub of foot powder, its label proclaiming, matter-of-factly, 'Robson's Foot Powder for Sweaty, Smelly Feet'. Got to love the Aussies.

The lodge itself was situated in Tasmania's high country and the large shallow lakes were bordered by eucalyptus forests and tussock. After another evening of great food and swapping fishing stories with the other guests, we had an early night, tired from the day's travel. I'd also planned to get up early. Jason had informed me that my guide for the trip, Lonsdale, was delayed and wouldn't be there until the afternoon. He advised me to try Big Jim Lake on my own in the morning, only a 50-yard stroll from the lodge itself. Here, he said, in the shallow margins, I would find trout 'fossicking', or tailing.

I don't like getting up early, even for fishing. I never have done much good getting up and getting out of the house at the crack of dawn. The transition from night to day always seems to go so quickly, rendering the whole experience a bit pointless. I far prefer the witching hour of dusk. Here, the anticipation and the odds of a result are far greater. With the coming of the day, I feel my chances, like the night, slipping away. When you're camped by the water its different, of course. You can rise just before dawn and make the most of the transition from dark to light.

I did manage to rise early that morning, though, and after a quick coffee grabbed my rod and made the short walk to the lake.

The ground was tightly packed red soil, sloping gently down to the water. A herd of kangaroos watched me curiously from the edge of a stand of eucalyptus trees. I approached the water cautiously. I was as much worried about treading on a snake as scaring off the trout. Crouching slightly, I made my way along the bank in the pale light of the early morning. The water was flat calm, and up ahead only feet from the bank I could see small rings on the surface, followed by the dorsal fin of a feeding trout.

What followed were two hours of frustration. With the fish so close in, it was hard to make short casts; I couldn't load enough line on the rod to propel the fly. Throw in overhanging trees, bushes and my relative inexperience at fly fishing, and I was struggling. Time and again I either cast too short or too long, putting the line over the fish and sending it bolting into deep water. Soon the sun was fully up and the magical first few hours of the day had gone.

I'm nothing if not tenacious, though, when it comes to fishing. Guessing the fish had moved into deeper water now, I waded into the lake as far as I could and began to search the water with a weighted nymph, making long casts and letting the nymph sink. I worked the fly tight to the bottom and began a slow figure-of-eight retrieve. After about a dozen casts I felt the line draw tight and the little 5-weight slammed over the line, fizzing through the fingers of my left hand. Fish on!

I played it to the shore, a beautifully marked brown trout of maybe 3lb. I unhooked him in the water, admired the vivid black and red spots and dark bronze flanks for a few seconds, then watched as it swam off, slowly at first, then disappearing into the depths with a flick of its tail.

I didn't know it then but that was the last trout I was going to catch in 'Tassie'. Lonsdale, our guide, no doubt tried his best but I never got to grips with the fishing there. We had fun trying, though. Once Lonsdale and I were off wading a shallow wood-filled pond. We had left Nathalie back at the main lake about a hundred yards away. She had waded out quite a distance and we could see her practising her casting. All of a sudden Lonsdale and I heard screams and commotion, and saw Nathalie speed-paddling back to shore. We ran to see what was happening. We saw Nathalie, gratefully on shore, though a little upset. She said she had been in the water when she spotted something moving out in the lake. As she waded out for a closer look, whatever it was out there started to come nearer. Then she saw it was a snake. No problem, though, it was still quite far away. Calm at this point, she placed the fly rod under one arm and reached in her pocket for the camera. The snake, now maybe anxious for a photo opportunity, made a beeline straight for her. It was at this point that the guide and I were alerted. Tasmania has three very venomous species of snake and, by the way Nathalie described it, Lonsdale said it could have been a tiger snake, one of the three. Nathalie cut back on the wading at that point in the trip.

One evening after dinner, one of the guides asked if we wanted to go on a night safari. After jumping in his big pick-up truck we made our way slowly through the bush, our path lit by a large lamp mounted on the roof. Kangaroos were everywhere. We also spotted a wombat, quite a shy, rare creature.

We had been driving in the bush for about an hour and were about to head back to the lodge when our driver spotted something up ahead. He slowed the big truck to a crawl and leaned over the wheel, straining to get a better view. 'Could be your lucky night,' he said.

The truck came to a halt in a clearing, with brown grass bordered by eucalyptus trees. Here, only yards from our front bumper, the lifeless body of a small kangaroo lay on the ground. Then, in a series of violent jerks, it moved. A small face appeared behind the 'roo. Jaws agape, its black fur stained with blood, we had gate-crashed a Tasmanian devil's dinner party. After a quick look in our direction and a few sniffs, the devil went back to its meal, seemingly untroubled by our presence. We watched, grimly fascinated. Rolling down the windows, audio was added to the visual, the devil snorting and snarling as it gored its unfortunate victim. Our guide explained the Tasmanian devils are scavengers as opposed to hunters and that it had probably come upon its meal when the 'roo was already dead. It would eat meat, fur and bone, wasting nothing. After a while, the excited banter gave way to a grim silence as the devil continued to gorge on the kangaroo. The guide put the truck into reverse and backed slowly away, letting nature take its course.

The next morning we packed up our stuff and got ready to leave. Tasmania had not been very productive for me on the fishing front but I was left with an impression of a beautiful, wild and unique place. OK, it has a dark history, but where on earth doesn't? Whereas the carnage of the Second World War has largely been forgotten in Europe with shiny new buildings and ever-increasing populations, in Tasmania's brooding quietness it's harder to forget history. Maybe it's just more honest.

It was time to head back to the UK. The fishing part of the trip was over but we still had a four-day stopover in Tahiti to look forward to. Looking back, it was truly the trip of a lifetime, the memories burned into my mind forever. Five countries visited, thousands of miles travelled, and this time I got to savour the experience of travel to new places and not have to pack up and move on to get to another show.

CHAPTER TEN

A River Twenty

'Bloody hell,' I said to myself. 'That was a decent mirror carp!'

It was a boiling hot day in August 1992 and I was preparing to cast my link-legered breadflake intended for chub. The carp had surfaced in midriver, lingering for a moment, almost lazily, then diving for the bottom with a slap of its tail. The river in question was the Colne, the little gem of a river that I was delighted to have on my doorstep. The Boyer Leisure-controlled stretch either side of the A40 was my haunt, and I plundered the chub and bream either quiver-tipping or trotting with breadflake.

Usually I would fish short sessions during the week, and rarely saw another angler, but did on one occasion meet another fisherman on the lower stretch, and he confirmed that I hadn't been imagining things when I saw that carp. 'Loads under the bridge, mate,' he said. 'There's one that's got stuck in a traffic cone – 'ad to grow around it.'

A tall story? Yep, but there might be a grain of truth in it, though a cone-shaped carp seemed slightly odd. Nevertheless, the information was locked away in the back of my brain.

I had got to know the river well, but I usually kept clear of the A40 bridge area. The bridge itself wasn't exactly a thing of beauty: dirty, yellow brick and grey concrete. The incessant din of traffic didn't add any charm, so I usually headed upstream. There, if you tried hard enough, you could pretend you were on the Hampshire Avon, as the river itself flowed hard and had luxuriant weed growth. Many happy hours were spent on the Colne and the Kennet, as I got the barbel bug. The years passed, I got more into carp fishing, mainly on the Croxley syndicate waters. In 2000, my music career perked up again and I began touring heavily, sometimes nine months out of the year. In 2001 we finished a particularly gruelling (it is hard work, honest!) tour in South America. I couldn't wait to get home and get the rods out again. Looking out of the window on the plane, day-dreaming of home and considering my options, I thought of those Colne carp.

It was by now late November and winter was starting to show its teeth. I wasn't too worried. A few years before, I'd lived and worked in Paris for three months and had caught loads of carp through the winter months from the small lakes in the Bois de Boulogne. The key was baiting. Keep the bait going in consistently and the carp would get on it. Sounds easy, and it is. The hard part is finding the right water. Nowadays, lakes in the UK with good carp stocks get fished year round. Not ideal for pre-baiting, as someone else is likely to cash in on your hard work. Miles and miles of rivers see very little angling pressure, however, so then it's down to locating the carp. I'd seen one or two fish near the road bridge and heard the odd rumour, as well as the one about the cone carp. So I decided to have a go. I would hedge my bets with the bait. I decided on Nash Tangee squids as they have a bit of a fruity flavour. I would supplement this with hemp, pellets and corn.

I visited the river every other day for two weeks, spraying bait under the bridge. With every visit my anticipation grew as I looked forward to wetting a line. It was sometime in February when I eventually pulled into the small slip road that runs along-side the river, towards the Anoopam Mission. In the car this time was not only bait but my rods. Today was the day.

I parked up, loaded my gear and trudged back up the road towards the bridge. A left turn at the top of the road saw me crossing the bridge itself via a narrow (make that very narrow) pavement that bordered the busy road. I made my way to the other side as the traffic thundered past just a few feet away. After clambering through a hole in the wooden fence, I walked down the few yards to the river. Feeling slightly disorientated by the noise of the road, I took a few moments to survey the river and gather my thoughts.

In the summer, the river is awash with rushes, lily pads, cabbages and streamer weed. A riot of green. Now though, stripped bare by winter, it showed the scars of an urban river. The lush sedges of summer were now withered and brown. Rubbish, hidden by growth then, clung to grasping low branches of trees. A Tesco carrier bag swayed in the current, just in front of me (caught on some underwater obstruction, probably a traffic cone). A bit further out a large tail waved . . . a carp! It was feeding, head down, ploughing up the bottom, sending plumes of silt that wafted slowly to where I stood downstream. As you do in these situations, I slowly bent my knees to a crouching position and backed away from the river in a slightly comical backwards Cossack dance, not even daring to change my facial expression, hoping the carp hadn't seen me. When I peeked again from behind a tree stump, the fish was still there. I set up well away from the bank. Nothing fancy rig-wise, 15lb braided hookweight, strong size-8 hook. I used a 2oz lead as the water was only three feet deep. As there was at least one carp present, I didn't want to cause too much disturbance. Mind you, these fish were used to articulated lorries speeding over their heads day and night.

I got the bait in position and sat back to await events. I didn't have to wait long, as after about only 20 minutes the near rod was away and I was attached to my first river carp. The fight was unspectacular and, after a short while, I slid a rather surprised-looking low double-figure mirror over the net cord. It's nice when a plan comes together (and it makes up for the many that don't). I thanked the carp, released him back into his river and told him to watch out for those nasty traffic cones. I fished on through the afternoon and into dark but had no more action. I packed up and headed home, chucking out some more boilies before I left.

I was back a few days later and by about 2pm I was set up and fishing. I had decided to fish the other bank on this occasion. The swim involved a slightly longer chuck through to reach the water under the bridge to my right.

I placed the first rod about a third of the way across and just in the shadow of the bridge. The second was cast to the far bank, near where I fished a few days previously. A few pouchfuls of boilies followed and I sat back to wait. The day was bone-chillingly cold with a battleship-grey sky and a sharp easterly wind. I hadn't brought a bivvy as I wasn't intending to spend the night, so thank God for thermal fishing suits and moonboots. I zipped up my coat and hunkered down, only my eyes exposed to the elements. Despite the grim conditions, I felt confident of some action. I knew the chub were still active and hoped if they were feeding it might encourage any carp present to join in too.

After a couple of hours I had a stuttering take on the rod. Lifting the rod, I felt minimal resistance: chub. I winched the fish towards me and engulfed it in my outsize landing net, where it lay, looking slightly undignified. It was a fat four-pounder, and I still had to admire its bronze flanks. I slipped the chevin back and re-cast the rod.

Afternoon had slipped into early dusk when the nearside rod burst into life. The little Fox Micron squealed and the blue light cut through the gloaming. I scrambled over to the rod, which was now hooped round at an alarming angle, and I disengaged the baitrunner. The rod slammed over as the fish continued to take line, heading under the bridge. The fight was epic. Every time I managed to gain line and pump him upstream, it would tear off downstream again. Eventually, I had the still unseen fish plodding around in front of me, sullen now, but still heavy and powerful. I managed to lift the fish slowly up from the bottom where I bundled it into the net at the first attempt.

It was fully dark now. I let the fish rest in the margins, still in the landing net, while I readied mat, scales and camera. With that done, I retrieved the fish and laid it on the mat. The torchlight revealed a decent common. I did weigh the fish – a little over 21lb but I don't remember exactly. I do remember feeling a real sense of satisfaction, as you do when you've undertaken something pioneering and it's paid off. Still buzzing the next day, I sent a picture off to the *Angler's Mail*. The following week, when I picked up a copy of the mag as usual, there was not only a picture of the carp, but a double-page spread on me and the band!

That was the last time I fished for those river carp. There were other fish to try for, and more gigs to do. I still live in the area, and drive over the bridge occasionally. Recently I decided to go and have a look, for old times' sake, though technically you're not supposed to be on that part of the river now. Things looked very different. Two new gravel pits have been dug in the adjacent fields and now a conveyer belt runs over the river, supported by a metal bridge, built to carry gravel to the waiting barges on the Grand Union Canal. On closer inspection the bridge was climbable so, from that vantage point, I could see the river more clearly. A shoal of bream, about a dozen in number, grazed slowly over the gravel bottom, shadowed by a large pike. I looked downstream where the dark water swirled under the bridge. I could just imagine a couple of big old carp lying-up in the sanctuary of the bridge overhead. One of them a slightly conical shape . . .

CHAPTER ELEVEN

Pike Fishing And Oasis

In the winter of 2002, Iron Maiden were holed up at Sarm Studios, west London, recording the *Dance of Death* album. Now, if you don't know anything about the band you could be forgiven for thinking that we (or at least one of us) have a fascination with death and the afterlife. Some may even think we're devil-worshipping, child-sacrificing heathens. It all sounds a bit serious but, of course, we're not really like that at all and we can be as daft as anyone. The *Dance of Death* album dealt with some pretty heavy themes, including war and death, but the sessions were offset by the sort of humour that most middle-aged rock musicians will understand. Songs such as 'Wildest Dreams' were referred to as 'Wildest Breams', 'No More Lies' became 'No More Pies', and so on. Childish, yes, but you're always looking for ways to break the tension when you are recording. The band are together in a confined space, and every nuance of your playing or singing is under the microscope. You're desperately hoping that the ideas that you've spent the past two months working on will come out sounding amazing – even compare to the bands you grew up idolising. So, in that atmosphere, a laugh and a joke go a long way.

Around this time, I had an urge to buy a boat. This was not a flight of fancy, as I had a specific purpose in mind for it. I'd asked in my local tackle shop about pike fishing locally to me. The guy in the shop (also called Adrian) had been telling me about a section of the Grand Union Canal that he match fished regularly.

'You wanna get on the gaps, mate,' he assured me.

The 'gaps' were literally that. A large marina on the far side of the canal was bordered by sections of long, thin, manmade islands that formed a barrier, and along this were several gaps. A deadbait lobbed just short of the gap had a good chance of being snaffled by a pike, Adrian told me. He added in a slightly lower voice and with an intense stare that the marina itself was stuffed full of all sorts of specimens.

'You can't fish there, though. Not allowed, mate. Gaps're the closest you can get,' he said before breaking off our conversation to serve someone some maggots.

So off I went. Armed with my pike gear and various dead-baits, I made my way to the aforementioned section of the Grand Union Canal. I've always had a soft spot for canals. Maybe it's a hint of nostalgia, a glimpse of the way things used to be . . .

This section was quite picturesque compared to the industrial canals of inner London where I grew up. On the towpath side there was a selection of barges, some well-maintained and others rusting and neglected. There were three main gaps on the far side of the canal and I headed for the furthest one, thinking it would be nice and quiet. I plonked my gear opposite the gap and surveyed the scene, and it did look good. You could just imagine the pike lying in wait in the gap for any passing unfortunate roach or bream. It was a lovely mild, overcast afternoon as I sent the first bait sailing across the water just short of the gap. I'd brought my rod pod and buzzer set-up, and was placing the rod in the rest and adjusting the bobbin when everything pulled up tight. Fish on already! The pike must have taken the bait on the drop. After a short fight, I landed a pike of 6lb or so. Not a monster, but there's always a sense of satisfaction when you achieve something you set out to do. A good start.

A cyclist was passing by on the towpath. Not one of those Lycra-clad, camera-wearing types, but an old boy with a rusty bike and a flat cap, pleasingly in keeping with the olde-worlde atmosphere of the canal. I stopped him and asked him if he would take a picture and he duly obliged.

'Cor, that's a big 'un!' he said.

It always amuses me when non-fishing folk see a decent-sized fish on the bank. They are genuinely quite excited. They have no idea of the size of the fish we have in our British waters. Perhaps in that moment they can understand why people fish.

I thanked the old boy and prepared another bait, and then something happened I just wasn't expecting. I was fishing in between two moored barges and now, in the barge to my right, I could hear banging and crashing. This noise suddenly changed into a rocksteady beat. A drummer was practising inside the barge! So much for peace and quiet. He wasn't half bad actually. I fished until the drummer had had enough, and on into quiet darkness as pike will happily feed at night. I didn't catch any more pike but experienced some quite violent jerks on the rods, one resulting in the rod being pulled off the rest. Despite this, after the initial indication, the bite never developed.

I headed home and spent the next week in between recording sessions thinking how I could fish the canal more effectively. I needed a boat. With a vessel, I could moor in the gap and fish into the marina itself. I thought back to an old episode of John Wilson's *Go Fishing* TV programme. In this one, he goes pike-fishing on an estate lake, using a collapsible boat. At the end of his session he simply folds up his boat and chucks it in the back of his car. This was what I needed. But where to find one? There was nothing on the internet. I searched the odd boating magazine, but nothing. I decided to go to the Earls Court Boat Show. I drove into London one Sunday afternoon and, after the usual shenanigans parking my car in the capital, I made my way to the show.

I got there just as they were beginning to shut things down, and after looking at some impressive ocean-going, luxury yachts, I spotted something familiar; in a small corner of the vast exhibition hall there was a stall set up, and on a stand in front was the foldaway boat that featured in the John Wilson programme. I couldn't believe my luck. I made my way over and got the attention of one of the guys who were in the process of dismantling the stand and packing up all the gear. I was told I needed to speak to John, and somebody called him over. He eyed me warily as we shook hands and I told him I was interested in a folding boat. He was probably trying to figure out if I was serious or just another punter with a load of daft questions,

'Three months,' he said.

'Excuse me?'

'The boat. Takes three months to build, if you want one.'

Three months? I wanted one now!

'What about the display model?' I asked.

He turned to look at the display model and then back to me. 'Well, it's a display model, innit?'

I eventually convinced him it would be a good idea for him to sell me his display model. I had brought £250 cash on the off-chance of finding a boat and he readily accepted my offer.

He showed me how to set up and dismantle the boat, then bade me goodbye. So there I was, in the middle of Earls Court

Exhibition Centre with a small boat that I needed to get back to my car, which wasn't close by . . .

The boat was an ingenious affair. It comprised a main hull of two parts, connected with a rubberised sheet. The whole lot folded out and was stabilised crossways with seats that clipped on forward, middle and . . . er . . . aft, I think.

The seats I carried under my left arm, and the main hull, which was about the size of two coffin lids (there you go, death again), under my right arm. Luckily there was a small wheel on the bottom of the hull so I half-carried, half-dragged the whole lot out of the Exhibition Centre and down the half a mile or so of Earls Court Road, where my car was parked. Thankfully the boat fitted into the back of my car once I had folded the rear seats down. My back ached and my arms were hanging off, but now possessed of a boat, I couldn't wait to launch her on the Grand Union Canal in pursuit of the pike.

I had work to do first, though, and was back in the studio on the following Monday and Tuesday to complete some guitar overdubs. I was joined on the Tuesday by Janick Gers, fellow member of the guitar cohort. During a break in recording, Jan and I went out into the studio recreation area to have a coffee. There were two studios at Sarm, and the door to the second studio opened out into the recreation area. At that moment the door opened and a figure emerged, clad in a parka, with spiky hair and wearing shades. He turned away and, arms swinging, he strutted monkey-like across the recreation area and up the stairs.

'All these young guys,' I tutted. 'They all think they're in Oasis!' Jan and I chuckled.

A few minutes later, said character made his way down the stairs but instead of going back to the studio he made a beeline for us.

'Iron Maiden,' he said. 'Fookin' respect!' and stuck out his hand.

It was none other than Liam Gallagher himself. He explained that he was here as Nicole Appleton (his future wife from the girl group All Saints) was recording with her sister in Studio 2. Now I, being a reserved kind of chap, would have been happy with a quick hello. Not so Janick.

'Come on,' said Jan. 'I'll show you round our studio.'

Liam was not keen, and I felt his pain. I'm never comfortable myself with going into another band's working space. You feel like an outsider. Jan was insistent, though, and Liam was persuaded. We all trooped into our studio and Liam did his best to appear impressed.

'This is all mine and Davey's guitars,' Jan said. 'Don't try anything, we've counted 'em all.'

Ouch. I winced inwardly. Liam didn't flinch.

The best part was the look on producer Kevin Shirley and Steve Harris's faces when we walked into the control room with Liam in tow. We played him a bit of one of the new songs and he nodded in time to the music appreciatively,

'Yeah,' he said. 'Fookin' 'eavy.'

He should've been a music critic.

With a day off on Wednesday, I planned my trip to the Grand Union Canal. The day dawned bright and very cold as I loaded the car with gear for the short trip to the canal. On arrival, I found a parking spot and set about carrying the boat, a few bits at a time, over the humpback bridge that spanned the lock. A set of stairs then had to be negotiated down to the towpath, where I leaned the bits against a wall. I then went to fetch another piece and the rest of my gear. My only worry was that some scallywag might nick something when I was back at the car as the canal towpath sees some, shall we say, 'characters', but all was well when I returned.

I then set about assembling the boat, which took a little time, but when completed seemed sturdy enough. Then it was time for the launch. I've always been wary of boats as things can go wrong very quickly if you don't know what you're doing.

The launch went well apart from the boat sitting a bit high in the water. I loaded my gear in the boat and rowed enthusiastically towards the first 'gap'.

I tied up one end of the boat to some bushes, the other end I secured to a long metal pole I had brought with me, which I drove into the soft bottom of the canal. This would put me side-on to the canal so I could cast into the marina itself.

I had only brought one rod, a nine-foot medium-action Daiwa model. I coupled this with a small baitrunner-type reel by Mitchell that has a bite alarm built in to it. Very clever. With this set-up I could sink and draw a deadbait, or just cast it out and let it sit static on the bottom.

LEFT Me aged around twelve with the Avon barbel.

BELOW Fast–forward twenty-odd years, my first 'proper' barbel. Caught from the River Kennet at Aldermaston.

ABOVE My dad in foreground, and me with my older sister Kathleen. The early 1960s at Tottenham Locks.

ABOVE Dave Murray on drums and me on guitar, circa early 1970s, jamming in the cellar of my house in Clapton. The guitar leaning against the wall behind me is the one I bought off Dave.

LEFT Dave Murray and I doing the obligatory 'daft teenagers in a photo booth' shots.

ABOVE An early line-up of Urchin. L–R: Maurice Coyne (guitar), Barry Tyler (drums), me (with fishing hat!), John Hoye (bass).

ABOVE Urchin band and roadies, late 1970s. Back row L–R: Maurice Coyne (guitar), Barry Tyler (drums), Terry Tyler, "Big Dave" Lewis. Front row L–R: Alan Levet (bass), me (guitar and vocals), Brian Gafney.

ABOVE Myself with ex-Maiden drummer and fishing partner, the late Clive Burr, on the road in the 1980s.

RIGHT Me with drummer Mr. Nicko McBrain, during rehearsals for the *Somewhere in Time* album. (Photo: Ross Halfin)

BELOW Me and my dad backstage at Hammersmith Odeon. (Photo: Ross Halfin)

LEFT A River Thames beast, 15lb 8oz!

RIGHT A 5lb 12oz chub from the River Kennet.

ABOVE A winter 'six' from the River Colne.

RIGHT A huge 7lb 14oz chub caught from the River Colne on the summer solstice in 2010.

ABOVE A River Colne upper 'nine'.

ABOVE Central Park, New York. 'If you can catch 'em there, you'll catch 'em anywhere...'

LEFT A nice peacock bass taken from a Miami canal during a break from band rehearsals.

LEFT Nathalie and I at Lake Louise, Canada.

RIGHT In Wells Gray Park, Canada. I was thinking that maybe a Camaro wasn't the best vehicle for heading off fishing on rough logging roads… Luckily, we only went about 15 feet before some trees broke our fall.

LEFT Skitchine Lake Lodge, Kamloops, Canada. 'We got bears, but they won't bother you.'

BELOW Afloat on the main lake at Skitchine, enjoying the solitude after the madness of the *Powerslave* tour.

ABOVE Returning a big rainbow trout to its home in Wells Gray National Park. It very nearly became lunch!

BELOW First place in Lahaina Wahine Jackpot tournament, won by Nathalie in Hawaii.

ABOVE Nathalie, playing a good trout on the Makarora River.

LEFT New Zealand was a beautiful, unspoiled fishing paradise.

RIGHT Aboard Dick Fraser's 'copter, heading off for another fishing adventure. Cedar Lodge, New Zealand.

LEFT The big Hunter River brown trout.

BELOW The same fish from a different angle showing the tremendous width across the back.

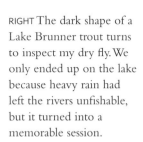

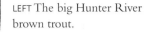

RIGHT The dark shape of a Lake Brunner trout turns to inspect my dry fly. We only ended up on the lake because heavy rain had left the rivers unfishable, but it turned into a memorable session.

LEFT Welcome to Tasmania!

ABOVE Looking for a 'fossicking' fish at London Lakes, Tasmania.

ABOVE RIGHT Picking the right fly with guide Lonsdale in Tasmania.

RIGHT We watched in grim fascination, as a Tasmanian devil tucked into his supper of kangaroo.

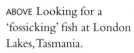

ABOVE The Grand Union Canal at Harefield, and the Gap where I had the pike haul.

RIGHT Last fish of a memorable day on the canal: a 17lb pike.

RIGHT An armful of sturgeon from the Fraser River in British Columbia, Canada.

BELOW A 21lb January common, from the Étang de Suresnes, Paris. The lake was conveniently close to Guillaume Tell Studios where we were recording the *Brave New World* album, and I had it all to myself during the early winter months of 2000.

LEFT A bulldozer of a carp. At 34lb, the big common took me by surprise on a busy spring afternoon in the Bois de Boulogne.

ABOVE A fat 13lb 6oz from the Colne on a wild and stormy night.

ABOVE Early success. A 7lb 4oz tench from the syndicate lake.

ABOVE A big bonus bream from a tench session 13lb 6oz.

ABOVE A perfect example of Tinca tinca: 8lb.

ABOVE A late season, 9lb 1oz.

RIGHT 12lb 2oz. They were getting bigger. Taken on trundled meat in the middle of a boiling hot August day from the River Colne near Uxbridge.

BELOW Settled in after the tench, for a long session on the British Carp Study Group's Korda Lake.

BELOW An absolute brute of a mirror carp of just over 40lb from Korda Lake.

BELOW Finally! The culmination of a ten-year quest. A beautiful tench of 10lb 8oz.

LEFT Patrick with his River Ebro common of 44lb.

BELOW My son Dylan with a River Ebro carp.

ABOVE Martin with his first Ebro carp.

RIGHT Me playing a barbel at Cromwell Weir, River Trent. The resident swan takes the opportunity to plunder my bait supplies. Dean's probably asking, 'How big?', and Lawrence concentrates on his rod tips.

RIGHT Bringing a River Ahr trout to hand, with Lutz offering expert local knowledge.

LEFT Dean Macey, Spug, and myself at Collingham on the River Trent – with the barbel that triggered the 'barbecue incident'. The fish remained oblivious to our evident amusement at the whole thing.

LEFT "Deano" with one of *three* 14lb barbel! All taken in a mad forty-five minute spell.

RIGHT On the way to a bonefish flat in the North Caicos by way of airboat. John Gill is at the controls. I'm grimacing partly because of the speed, but mostly because of the noise of the engine. (Photo: Craig Walker)

LEFT A Turks Islands bonefish of 7lb caught at close quarters in inches of water. I've caught bigger fish, but haven't had scales with me at the time. I'm still after that magical 'double' though. (Photo: Craig Walker)

BELOW Me pointing to Robert Palmer's old house at Compass Point, Bahamas. I had a layover in Nassau and decided to pay a visit.

RIGHT Wading back to the kayak after an evening's pursuit of bonefish. The flats have an atmosphere and charm all of their own.

RIGHT Dave and I waiting to board Ed Force One at Stansted, about to embark on 2008's *Somewhere Back In Time* tour.
(Photo: John McMurtrie)

ABOVE Having fun onstage on the *Final Frontier* tour, Perth, Australia. The Les Paul Gold Top I'm playing was my first 'proper' guitar. I bought it when I was eighteen with money earned from a summer working on a building site. L–R: Bruce Dickinson, me, Steve Harris, Dave Murray and Janick Gers. (Photo: John McMurtrie)

LEFT Over the years, I've found a way to combine my passion for music and fishing.
(Photo: John McMurtrie)

ABOVE Touring the world in a jumbo jet does tend to attract attention…

ABOVE Myself and Nathalie flanked by daughters Brittany (far left) and Natasha (far right). (Photo: John McMurtrie)

LEFT Touring's hard work, honest! (Photo: John McMurtrie)

BELOW Making my way to the stage in Madrid with our production manager Patrick Ledwith, during the *Legacy* tour. (Photo: John McMurtrie)

I decided on a static approach first, mounting a small dead trout, lobbing it just a few yards from the boat into the marina itself. The bait took a while to hit bottom, which was a good sign. If the marina was deeper than the adjacent canal, I suspected that the roach and bream would have moved in there for the winter, hopefully followed by the pike.

I sat back and poured a cup of tea from my flask. It was a pleasant February morning and I was enjoying my day so far. Or I was – until I looked down and noticed water in the bottom of the boat. Quite a lot of water. The boat must have had a leak somewhere. Quickly emptying the contents of my bait bucket onto the front seat, I improvised a bailer and managed to get most of the water out in a few minutes. As long as I did this every half an hour or so, I thought I would stay afloat. Luckily I had donned my wellies so I was still dry. Nothing worse than cold, wet feet when you're fishing.

Looking into the gap itself, I could see it was festooned with old timbers and metal poles. These must have been remnants from the barrier that existed previously. That certainly ruled out trying to fish into the marina by casting across from the towpath side. A hooked fish would stand no chance of being pulled back through the gap full of snags. But here I was, sitting pretty, if slightly wet, in my new boat. Just then there was a series of bleeps and the rod was dragged along the boat, coming to a stop at the front. Something had picked up the deadbait. This is for me the most exciting part of pike fishing, the *Jaws* moment.

I picked up the rod and tightened down. A nodding of the rod tip confirmed a fish was there. A sweeping strike and the fish was on! It didn't feel like a monster but at least it was some action on this cold day. A few minutes later, I netted a beautifully marked and well-conditioned pike of about 7lb. I removed the barbless treble and admired him for a second, then slipped him back to his watery home. Nowadays I use a single large hook for piking as they are generally a bit easier to work with than trebles. Using this set-up, and striking quickly after the fish has picked up the bait, lessens greatly any possible damage to the fish. Pike can quickly gorge a bait and it's better to miss a few than deep-hook a fish. What followed was one of the best piking sessions I have ever experienced. I caught pike after pike on the static bait, all small though, between 5 and 7lb.

About 40 yards across the marina were the mooring jetties with multiple crafts tied up there. There was one barge in particular that I kept looking at. I could just imagine a big old pike lying under there. A cold-eyed killer queen digesting her last victim. I only had my little spinning rod but I thought if I mounted my biggest deadbait I might have enough weight to make the cast to that barge. I selected a bait, lined up the cast and propelled it with all my might towards the spot. I'd miscalculated a bit because not only did it reach the barge, but it smashed into the hull. Luckily though, the bait slid down the side and plopped into the water right underneath the barge: perfect. Bite, I thought.

My pulse raced in anticipation of a take, but the bait made it back to me unscathed. Another cast was launched, this time to the front of the barge. This landed perfectly and, just as I had taken up a little slack line, there was a tremendous wrench on the rod and a huge swirl under the front of the barge. The pike tried to dive under the hull but I managed to steer it out into open water. The fish just plodded around in the deep water as I stood with rod bent double in the boat. This felt like a big fish. I drew it nearer and it came to the surface a few yards away. As it came past the boat, it turned on its side and kind of looked at me. Then, with a tremendous surge of power, it went through the gap and out into the canal. It was big all right, certainly a new personal best. After some more to-ing and fro-ing, I managed to net the big girl. Yes! What a day's fishing.

'That's a nice one!' a voice called out.

I looked up and saw the owner of one of the boats that were moored up on the towpath side. He must have been watching proceedings. I asked if he would take a photo for me, and I upped anchor and rowed back across the canal. The fish, unhooked, sulked in the large landing net, which was draped over the side of the boat. It weighed 17lb. Not a huge fish but a fine specimen all the same and one that was very satisfying. I'd put a lot of planning and effort into catching that pike. It was an impressive beast.

It was getting dark by now. I rowed back to the lock, moored up and began the process of packing up. With the car loaded to the rafters. I sat behind the wheel and started the engine, eager to get the heater going. I turned on the radio and it was playing 'Wonderwall' by Oasis. Honest . . .

CHAPTER TWELVE

Sturgeon And Falling Over In Vancouver

In 2008 I was on the road again, this time for the *Somewhere Back in Time* tour, which had us travelling through North America for two months. Looking at the tour itinerary I saw that we had a day off in Vancouver, British Columbia. Plans were drawn up for a trip out sturgeon fishing as the Fraser River, famous for the species as well as big salmon and trout, runs only 50 miles east of Vancouver.

Now, the first thing is that you don't want to be messing around trying to fish for sturgeon on your own. They run big and inhabit the sort of places that would need a sturdy boat, and an equally sturdy guide. So after a quick look around on the interweb, I found 'Fred's Guiding Service'. From the website, it looked like it was a professional-looking outfit with a small fleet of jetboats and a roster of guides. When I called them up, the lady on the phone said their staff were all very experienced and all but guaranteed I'd catch a sturgeon. Even if I wasn't in the charge of old Fred himself, I'd still 'have an awesome trip'. Awesome indeed. Mind you, in North America, everything seemingly has the potential to be awesome.

Trip booked, it was just a matter of hiring a car to drive the 50-odd miles from the hotel to the river. A quick call to the car hire company and it was job done.

Before the trip, the show in Vancouver was memorable on two counts. Firstly for the enthusiasm of the fans: they were amazing and really spurred us on. Sometimes during some of the older songs that we've played a million times, you can slip into autopilot, but with an audience like that it makes the whole thing come alive and feel fresh again.

Yes, I was enjoying myself on stage that night, hamming it up and showing off. Then, in the middle of 'The Trooper', while moving back towards the drum riser without looking, I tripped over Dave Murray's guitar lead and knew I was falling. This is a moment all rock stars dread. You know it's going to happen to someone in the band during the course of the tour, but will it be you? I've been 'over' a few times in my career and it always feels the same, like it's happening in slow motion. As you realise you are going to fall, it's 'Oh shit!' and down you go.

Of course, the more bombastic the show, the greater the embarrassment. In Vancouver, having been 'giving it the big 'un', my mortification was acute.

Now, when someone takes a tumble onstage, unless it's an obviously painful one, the remaining upright band members – as per tradition – gather round to laugh and point. That night, I just lay there and kept playing until a gap in the music allowed me to get up and carry on. Only now I felt like I was wearing a large hat that said 'I'm a Prat' in big letters. But don't gloat too much, chaps: it could be you tomorrow.

Show over, it was back to the hotel and a quick meet-up and a drink in the bar with my brother-in-law Marc Dufresne and his wife Quottnim, who'd flown in from their home in LA to visit old friends and catch the show. 'Did you fall over tonight?' Marc asked. We had a good catch-up and a nice bottle of wine and, before I knew it, it was 2am and they were calling last orders. I said my goodbyes and retired to bed. No such thing as an early night on the road, even for brave sturgeon fishers.

Next morning, I was up at the crack of 10am to the news that there was a problem with the hire car. They couldn't supply me with my original request for a middle-sized boring automatic Ford Royale. (Why do these mundane vehicles have such grand names? How about a Ford Bland-ola or a Vauxhall Boring As Shite, in overcast grey.) They assured me I was, in fact, getting an upgrade in the shape of a brand new fire-engine-red Ford pick-up truck. Oh well . . .

At least I had some transport, even if I had to run the gauntlet as tour managers Ian Day and Steve Gadd were waiting for me down in the lobby.

'Bloody 'ell! Where's the fire?' Ian shouted over in his Brummie brogue as I drove off.

Soon it was forgotten as I started to leave Vancouver and headed east towards Chilliwack, where I had arranged to meet my guide. After an hour of driving, I pulled off the freeway, where I caught my first glimpse of the Fraser. 'Mighty' is a much overused term when people describe rivers, but it was an apt description of this particular waterway. From where I stood on a bluff overlooking the river, you could see a good mile or two upstream. The river cascaded through a steep valley, studded with evergreens. White boulders split the heavy current to form large green pools of slack water. It was in these quiet spots, I imagined, that vast sturgeon would be lying in wait for any food items washed downstream in the flow. I was just about to leave when a huge fish leapt clear of the water and re-entered the river with a sound like a fridge being thrown into a swimming pool. If a memory is like a photo in the mind, I have a snap of that great fish: long, with a grey armoured back, its cream-coloured belly exposed as it twisted in the air, all set against an ideal picture postcard backdrop. I actually took a step back. Now I knew what I was dealing with. Talk about river monsters.

Once back in the car, it was only a few more miles to the rendezvous with my guide for the day. I pulled off the road and made my way down a rough, hilly track that led to the river. A bit further on, the land flattened out as it joined the river. There was a large dock, which housed a number of sleek-looking boats and the usual bait, tackle and hamburger joint. The kind of place where the proprietor will sell you a tub of worms and a cheese-burger, and then put them in the same bag.

There was a young guy tending to a boat. He was dressed in a baseball cap, fish-logoed hoodie and waders. When another chap called out to him and called him Brad, I knew he was my man. I've lost count of the number of guides I've fished with called Brad. Guides as a species can vary greatly and I've been lucky enough to fish some incredibly exotic places on guided trips. The best guides are cheerful without being overbearing, and will quickly judge your skill level and advise accordingly. They will have just enough anecdotes and conversation to make the day enjoyable and keep things moving along. On the other hand, a day stuck on a boat with someone you don't get on with can be torturous. On one particular day's bonefishing in the Turks and Caicos Islands, I was with a guy who hardly said a word all day and just sullenly poled me around the flats. To make matters worse, we didn't even see, let alone catch, any bonefish. That in itself is OK, apart from the fact that he charged me a small fortune.

Brad seemed like a good-enough guy, and I particularly liked the way he said, 'You ready to catch some sturgeon?' after we had introduced ourselves. Any worries about further small talk were averted as he gunned the boat's jet engine to life and turned up AC/DC's 'Highway to Hell' full blast. The boat had a pretty decent stereo system, apparently. The jetboat was fast and in no time we had reached our first spot. Here a side stream entered the main river, creating a tempting array of slack water, creases, deep pools and all manner of fishy-looking spots.

We anchored the throbbing boat and, with some hand signals and a little shouting, I communicated to Brad that it might be a good idea fishing-wise if we turned the music down a bit. (I think Sabbath's 'Iron Man' was blaring out at this point.) Bradley obliged and proceeded to ready the tackle, which as you'd expect was pretty beefy. Two catfish rods cut down to give them a bit more 'grunt', paired with multiplier reels loaded with 80lb braid. A triangular lead weight of 8oz was threaded on the line below that, and a trace of 50lb mono attached to a size-2 circle hook. One rod was baited with salmon eggs encased in a sack made of women's tights, the other with a piece of cut fish. These were then lobbed or lowered into likely looking spots, and the rods leaned up against the gunwale. When I remarked that surely the rods would be dragged in on the take, I was surprised to learn that the bite of a sturgeon was quite subtle. A few taps on the rod tip would indicate the sturgeon was mouthing the bait, followed by a steady draw as it moved off.

He had no sooner finished speaking when I noticed a slight movement of the rod. I was instructed to pick up the rod and wait until I felt the weight of the fish before striking. I duly obliged and was still yet to strike when Brad produced one of those game-fishing harnesses and instructed me to put it on. But before I could, the rod slammed over and the fish was on!

I had never felt such power. The fish just headed off for the main river and I couldn't do anything to stop it. Meanwhile, Brad settled down and started rolling a smoke. This was probably going to take a while.

'He'll probably jump,' said Brad between puffs.

Sure enough, the sturgeon breached: a five-foot monster suspended in midair only feet from the boat.

'Looks like you've got yourself a hundred-pounder.'

It's a bit different to gudgeon bashing at Tottenham Locks, I thought.

Eventually the fish began to tire and I brought him alongside the boat. At this point, I wondered how the hell we were going to get him onboard.

For Brad, meanwhile, it was business as usual. He casually pushed a button which released some kind of pulley mechanism to which was attached a large, heavy-duty, but soft plastic sling. This was then lowered to water level, the fish guided in, then hoisted on to the boat.

'You wanna picture?' said Brad, smiling.

Might as well, I thought. *It's not every day you get this close to a 100lb sturgeon.*

Grip and grin shot completed, the fish was tagged and lowered back into the cool waters of the Fraser River, where it disappeared with a defiant thrash of its huge tail. The tagging helps to track fish movements in the river system, which in turn helps the fish and game authorities keep up water quality and monitor spawning habitat.

Back on the boat, I was in a bit of a state. In fact, halfway through the fight, my arms had started aching so much that I was worried that it might affect my gig the following night in Calgary. It didn't, as it turned out. I didn't fall over either.

CHAPTER THIRTEEN

Parisienne Carpways

During the late autumn of 1999, work commitments required for me to uproot and move to Paris. 'Shame!' I hear you say. But not for me the bright lights of the Champs-Élysées or the flesh-pots of Pigalle, but a rather ordinary suburb, Suresnes.

It was a rather grey late October afternoon as I was trans-ported by taxi from Charles de Gaulle Airport. I wasn't really looking forward to being away from home and the wife and kids for the next three or four months. All my possessions were in the boot, including fishing gear. Surely there wasn't much fishing in Paris, but that's rock 'n' roll. To be honest, I was feeling a bit sorry for myself, staring out of the taxi window watching the rather dull Paris suburbs pass by. My mood brightened some-what as we drove into what appeared to be a park (although London born and bred I'm a country boy at heart). Ten minutes later we were still in the 'park'. *Some park this*, I thought.

'Where are we?' I asked the driver, in a mixture of French, English and hand signals.

'This,' he said proudly, 'is the Bois de Boulogne.'

'Blimey, I thought Boulogne was a port.'

He then proceeded to give its history. As he rattled on in French (mistakenly thinking I could understand more than the odd word), I did what I always do in these situations: look through the trees for signs of water.

Then I saw it. An unmistakeable glint. As we sped along, it turned into a fully fledged lake. Not quite your classic French carp heaven but it would be a start. I could even see a few anglers dotted around the edge.

'Is this Suresnes?' I groped hopefully in English but with a French accent.

'Oui, monsieur.'

'Yes!'

The hotel was only another two minutes further. I checked in, dropped my bags off and was back down in reception in double-quick time, wanting to have a recce before it got dark. A quick walk over the bridge (the River Seine ran by the hotel) and I was back at the lake. Bordered on two sides by busy roads, the lake extended to about six acres. The banks were well manicured with grass lawns stretching down to the water's edge. Large elm trees planted at intervals around the lake and park benches provided rest for the tired legs of Parisians out for a Sunday stroll.

There was only one real feature on the whole lake, right in the middle: the gnarled limbs of a huge sunken tree protruded up through the tea-coloured water. This was getting better all the time! But I still didn't know if the lake held carp. Well, if you don't ask, you don't get, so I made a beeline for the anglers I had seen from the taxi earlier. On closer inspection they were an odd bunch. In fact, only one of the men was actually fishing. He sat, face a study in concentration, eyes glued to a tiny float only a few feet from the edge. The rest of the mostly older gentlemen of the group stood behind, talking and smoking. When the angler landed a tiny roach there would be much laughing and comments directed towards '*le pêcheur*' in a display of good old-fashioned piss-taking. I don't know the French for 'taking the mick' but that is what they did.

As I watched, one by one they took turns with the brightly coloured pole until they had a plastic shopping bag full to the brim with fin-perfect roach, all about two inches long. The rod was then packed away followed by more talking, laughing, smoking and now drinking as they discussed their catch. This was a ritual I was to see many times at the lake, even on the bitterest days of January and February. I'm generally a laidback sort, not given to striking up conversations with total strangers. Except when it comes to gathering all-important carp information.

'Bonjour,' I offered.

The group fell silent and looked at me for a moment. The focal point of the gathering was a huge, white-bearded chap whose booming voice I had heard from a good 60 yards away when I was approaching.

'Bonjour,' he said, nodding, friendly enough.

'Pêcheurs!' I smiled, throwing in a few fishy hand signals 'What kind of . . . er . . . pêche,' I said, hands frantically doing fin movements, 'dans la . . . er . . . lake?' They seemed to understand.

I don't pretend to speak French but I do know a bit and have found that if you make an effort to speak the lingo, the locals will meet you halfway, chipping in with any English they know. They confirmed the presence of tench, roach, *silure* (catfish) and bream.

'La carpe?' I asked hopefully.

'Oui, oui, oui, la carpe!' At which point the big fella spread his arms wide and boomed, 'La grosse carpe!'

So, I had located a lake that held carp a few minutes from my apartment and within sight of the Eiffel Tower!

The next morning was spent visiting the local tackle shop (which I found in the *Yellow Pages*) to pick up some bait, licences and bits and pieces. The shop didn't have much in the way of carp gear, although the staff did confirm the presence of carp in the lakes and also kindly gave me the phone number of a chap they said was something of a local expert. On the way home, I popped into the shopping mall at La Défense and was pleasantly surprised to find that the sports department store Decathlon had an excellent fishing section. I picked up some much needed terminal tackle and a large quantity of Nash Tutti Frutti boilies. With the weather growing harsher, I figured this would be as good as anything for a baiting campaign.

Meanwhile we worked at Studio Guillaume Tell on what was to be the *Brave New World* album. I had recently re-joined the band, along with Bruce Dickinson, after a nine-year hiatus. During this time I'd undertaken a number of various musical projects, I'd recorded two albums with my band Psycho Motel (*State of Mind* and *Welcome to the World*) and collaborated with Helloween's Michael Kiske on two songs for his first solo album *Instant Clarity*. In 1996 Bruce asked me to join his band and I spent the next two years touring and recording with him.

If I was a bit surprised at the call from Bruce, it was nothing compared to hearing from Maiden manager Rod Smallwood in 1999. 'Bruce is going to re-join Maiden. Would you be interested?'

Since I had joined Bruce's band, fans had been asking if we were going to hook up with Maiden again. I always said I couldn't imagine it, and anyway it would be disrespectful to Blaze Bayley, who had taken over from Bruce, to even talk about it, and it didn't feel right to ask Janick Gers, who had replaced me, to step aside. But as the millennium approached, the stars seemed to be aligning. There was, though, a period of uncertainty. A lot of old feelings and emotions rose up again. Maybe it would just be one tour, where Janick and I would play half a set each? Also, although I'd agreed in principle to the idea, I hadn't heard anything definite back from the band. Maybe they were worried about my attitude. It hadn't been that positive by the end of my first tenure with Maiden. But I felt I was a different person now. I had a wife, children. I'd recorded, produced and sung on solo albums, worked with and learned from lots of great musicians. I was more confident, I'd grown up. Finally the call came, 'You're in.'

So here we were in Paris.

The first few days of recording were a little tense, to be honest. Was this going to even work? Three guitarists? Also, our new producer, Kevin Shirley, was trying to establish his authority, so there was a bit of 'cock fighting' going on. After a while, though, things settled down. I think the first thing we recorded was 'The Wicker Man', a straight-ahead rocker that myself and Bruce wrote. We did several takes of the song, then all trooped into the control room to have a listen. Obviously, you hear the track in headphones while you're actually recording, but the headphones are just for 'monitoring' so you don't really get the full picture until you listen back on proper speakers in the control room. We were all knocked-out with what we heard. The drums sounded huge and the guitars sounded powerful. We knew then that things were going to work. All this, and a lake full of carp, a few minutes away. Life was good.

My first few sessions on the lake produced only a few line bites, which at least proved there was some fish in the swim. I was fishing with two rods, with bait close to the main snag on either side, one with the Tutti Frutti and the other with a fishmeal in case the catfish were still active. Work proved hectic for the next couple of weeks and I didn't do much fishing. However, I still managed to get over to the lake every other day and kept the Tutti's going in and around the snag, and I also baited a few other back-up spots. The lake had little in the way of bottom features and, after plumbing up it, seemed to have an even depth of four or five feet throughout, so I felt confident the snag would hold fish in the winter.

The weather turned slightly milder, hovering just above freezing. I had endured a few sessions during blizzard conditions, drawing strange looks from the dog walkers and strollers.

'Carpiste?' or 'Anglais?' they would enquire.

'Oui,' I'd reply.

'Ah,' they would respond, as if understanding, before walking on.

It was now mid-November as I trudged laden with gear from my apartment to the lake. (I hadn't yet got round to hiring a car.) I was perspiring heavily when I reached the snag swim, always a good sign in the winter. The mild south wind blowing down the lake boosted my feeling of confidence. As usual I set up my 2½lb telescopic carp travel rods and baited one with fishmeal boilie and one with Tutti Frutti. Each rod was placed tight to the snag; the baitrunners, loaded with 12lb, were of 'locked up' style; rigs were running legers and barbless hooks, just in case a fish dived in the snag as I didn't want it to become tethered. Hook lengths consisted of a simple length of 15lb braid with a half-inch hair. Having not seen another carp angler on the lake, I didn't think the fish would be rig shy. I sat right on the rods and fished the bobbins on a six-inch drop.

I had arrived at the lake about an hour before dark, planning to fish for an hour or two into the night. I was vaguely aware of night-fishing not being allowed but I had little choice, having to work during the day. Anyway, I was tucked away behind a large elm tree. I had fired around 20 boilies in and around the snag on my arrival, hoping to stir the fish and get them feeding.

As I sat contentedly under the elm, I saw a big carp head and shoulder in the moonlight, sending large ripples lapping towards my bank. I have always found this a good sign, as opposed to carp splashing noisily or leaping clear of the water. A short while later, the bobbin rose steadily to the butt and I struck immediately into a heavy weight. A moment of stalemate followed as I held the fish hard, then a slight ease in pressure and a satisfying kick. It came away from the snag, into open water, then it was just a case of playing the fish out. After several powerful runs, I knotted the fish and swung it onto the mat. At 17lb, the pretty mirror was immensely satisfying for me. It represented the result of many blanks and a lot of work pre-baiting, all of which I enjoyed. The carp was just the punchline.

Indeed, over the next few weeks I was to land a dozen more from that swim, all on short evening sessions, the best a long common a shade over 20lb. The rest averaged mid-doubles. Pretty good fishing for early winter in the middle of a major city!

December the 20th saw me jetting home for Christmas and some much needed catching-up with the wife and kids. As time went on into the new year, I often thought about l'Étang de Suresnes – the Pond of Suresnes. Would the fish still be active or would they have shut-up shop as there had been no bait going in for about three weeks? Upon my return to Paris I was greeted with the sight of the lake under three inches of ice. This had been preceded by the worst storms in recent years and the Bois de Boulogne looked like a battle zone, with huge fir trees down everywhere and cars crushed by huge fallen elms.

Fishing was impossible at this point. A few days later, however, the weather changed for the better as a mild front swept into Paris. I arrived at the lake on a pleasant Friday after-noon. The snag swim was still under a thin layer of ice but large areas of the lake were clear. Indeed, the motley crew I had met on the first day were at the lake. The large fellow with the white beard greeted me cheerfully.

'Ah, carpiste!'

'Bonjour,' I offered, staring past him to where one of his mates seemed to be vigorously plucking some kind of bird.

'Il fait froid,' he said, gesturing to the lake.

But I had a free afternoon and I was going to fish. Anyway, I reasoned, after the big freeze, the fish would be hungry. After lobbing in some big stones to break up the thin remaining ice, I felt strangely confident. As I tackled up, a mild south-westerly breeze started up, pushing huge remaining sheets of ice down to the end of the lake. A fine rain began to fall, hastening the melt-down. After an hour with both rods out, the ice had all but melted; then the indicator rose steadily (I didn't get many 'screamers') and I was into my first ever January carp.

The procedure was becoming familiar now: clamp down hard, feel the fish kick, then yield as I brought it away from the snag into open water. A few minutes later I was admiring my best Suresnes carp so far, a dark 21lb mirror. So, the fish were still on the bait. A fact proved by the landing of a 10lb mirror later that evening and a clonking 21lb common the next day.

I continued to catch fish on every occasion. I fished short sessions throughout January and February, even on evenings when my landing net was frozen to the ground. Sometimes takes would occur within minutes of casting out. In total that winter, I took 25 carp from that swim with only one repeat capture, a common of 8lb. The average weight was approximately 17lb. Often the fish would be excreting the bait on the mat.

In fact, the fishing got a little too predictable, prompting me to try another, smaller lake, Étang de Longchamp, a short distance away. The same procedure was followed; heavy baiting around far-bank snags with the Nash Tutti-Fruttis every other day for a week. This lake was characterised by being long and narrow. It was also bordered by a busy road much frequented by 'ladies of the night'! The carp didn't seem to mind though.

On my first daytime session on the lake, I met a local carp angler who was just out for a stroll. He said he fished the Seine and had caught some fish up to 30lb locally. He also said I was wasting my time at this particular swim as all the carp were caught at the other end of the lake where there was a large bed of dead lilies. Of course, the inevitable happened; the alarm screamed, the rod hooped round and I was into another angry Parisienne carp, this time a scrappy 13lb mirror. I went on to land another dozen or so carp from Longchamp over the next couple of weeks. All the takes came from exactly the same spot, a small gap in the far-bank cover. Baits placed anywhere else were ignored. For the record, the carp of Longchamp averaged smaller than their Suresnes brothers, about 13lb.

On my return to England, I couldn't wait for the next winter as I really thought I'd got this winter-carping lark sussed. The reality was quite different, as what I had in Paris was a unique set of circumstances: a lake close to where I lived and therefore easy to keep the bait going in; a lake of even depth with a good stock of carp; and a location made easier by the presence of that one major snag in the middle of the lake. Also the fish were unpressured. A lake like that in London or the Home Counties would be lined with anglers year round. However, I have had some success in more out-of-the-way venues back home, such as underfished sections of rivers and overlooked, overgrown small pits. Not big fish by French standards, but worth a go if you are in the area and have some time to kill, or you're on a romantic weekend with the wife. Well, perhaps not the latter.

On my travels once again later that year, I found myself with a day off and decided to pass through Paris and spend the day at the lake in Suresnes. By now it was early May, and the weather was gloriously warm. About six other anglers were fishing, including a couple of carp boys. Amazingly the snag swim was free so I settled there and cast out two Tutti-Fruttis either side of the snag as usual. As I sat back enjoying the sun in T-shirt and shorts, I reflected on how different the lake was with the trees now in leaf and lily pads starting to show along it margins. The park was very busy with children, dogs and their owners. In a curious way it had lost some of the magic of the past winter when I had fished there alone in all weathers.

I was stirred from my reverie by a screaming alarm and the sight of the right-hand rod heading off the rests towards the lake at 100mph as I had forgotten to secure the butt properly. I was also a little further from the rods than usual. This necessitated me making a full lunging dive, Klinsmann-style, towards the disappearing rod. I managed to grab the rod and stop the fish from reaching the snag, almost dislocating my thumb in the process. As I scrambled to my feet, I was convinced I was playing my first 30lb carp. The fish tired easily and I soon realised I was way out on my first estimate. I slid the net under a mirror of about 4lb!

When I unhooked the fish, I soon became aware that a crowd had gathered. I squirmed. They must have witnessed the whole ridiculous episode. To make matters worse, there at the front was the big man with the white beard. Beside him was a small weasel-like fellow with what appeared to be the tail of a small jack pike sticking out of his trouser pocket.

'Carpiste,' he boomed. 'That's the smallest I've ever seen from here.'

Like they say, never go back.

But of course I did . . . again. In the winter of 2014 I again found myself in Paris, this time for the recording of *The Book of Souls* album. We had decided to record once again at Studio Guillaume Tell. We all met at the studio on a wet Monday afternoon. The place hadn't changed a bit. As we sat round on flight cases chatting while the roadies (sorry, technicians) scurried about plugging in amps and restringing guitars, we paused for reflection.

Almost fifteen years had passed since we had reunited and recorded the *Brave New World* album here. The time seemed to have gone by in a flash but we had achieved and done so much. We'd toured the world literally numerous times by road, boat and air. We'd played to enormous audiences from London to the USA, the Far East to Australia and New Zealand. The band had continued to grow and I'd been determined to savour every minute of it. I won't say I didn't have my down moments but they were far, far outweighed by the ups. I'd been given a unique opportunity, a second bite of the cherry. The band, for the most part, was playing better than ever, and with the introduction of in-ear monitors I was really enjoying playing live. I could hear myself! And I could hear the rest of the band too. That may sound strange but, back in the old days, the sound on stage in arenas was a lottery, with maybe one out of four having what I considered a good sound.

So here we were, back at Guillaume Tell all this time later. This was to be the band's sixteenth studio album. Recording went pretty smoothly and we had such a glut of material it ended up being a double album.

I had, of course, stashed my fishing gear in among the musical equipment that had come over by truck from the UK. I had a couple of Nash Hooligun 1¾ test-curve rods fitted with baitrunners, and about 10kg of Nash Tangerine Dream boilies and an assortment of end tackle, mat, seat and net, which I'd packed into an old suitcase.

In between recording sessions I had been trickling the bait into the lake at Suresnes. It hadn't changed much. The main snag that I had fished all those years ago, however, was barely visible above the surface of the shallow lake. There were some new snags, though. Some large trees had fallen in the water at the windward end of the lake. It looked like they had been there some time and, with it still being early spring and quite cold, I thought there was a good chance the fish might be laying up in there.

Over the next week or two, I peppered the snag with the Nash boilies and tins of sweetcorn. With recording going well, we decided to take a few days off. It was a Sunday when I made my way to the lake, loaded down with gear. The weather had been quite warm for the past few days and the park was crowded with dog walkers, joggers and screaming toddlers enjoying the sunshine. I must admit I didn't feel very confident as I set up that day. I had intended to fish a peg directly opposite the new set of snags, but a group of noisy teenage girls had taken up residence there so I moved 20 yards up the bank. This would mean that my lines would be at a slight angle to the snags, not ideal, but as I would be close to the rods, so I thought I could land any fish hooked safely. I didn't know for sure if there were any carp present in the lake these days, After all, I hadn't fished here for almost 15 years.

I baited each rod and cast both across and slightly to the left towards where the outermost branches of the sunken tree protruded, claw-like, just above the surface. I'd attached a small PVA bag of crushed boilies to each hookbait, hoping the scent would attract any fish out of the snags. I placed the rods on a buzzer bar 'T' with just one bank stick set-up, and rested the butts on the ground. Not the most secure set up, but you have to make some compromises when living out of a suitcase.

The day wore on and got warmer, and the crowds increased. I'd just got up to stretch my legs when, for the umpteenth time, a family came along the narrow path complete with obligatory boisterous dog. 'Bonjours' were exchanged as I made room for them to pass. I've seen some anglers get upset in these situations but there really is no point, as it's a public place and we're all entitled to enjoy it. Just as they exited my swim, I thought I heard the bite alarm sound. I was about ten yards from the rods, and I turned to see the left-hand rod now at a crazy angle as an angry carp made off with the bait. I was on the rod in a flash. The little Nash Hooligun was bent at full compression as I fought to keep the fish out of the snags. There was a temporary stalemate but eventually, by clamping down on the spool and walking backwards, I managed to get the fish away from danger. There was trouble in store, though.

The fish began to kite into the near left-hand margin, which was lined with bushes, some of which had branches extending into the water. I wound frantically but couldn't get any real purchase and the fish, obviously a very good one, made it into some sunken branches. As quickly as I could, I took off my shoes, rolled up my trousers, net in hand, and waded out into the lake. The water was cold, despite the sun, and I made my way towards where the line had caught on the bushes. I was a bit wary at this point. Such was the power of the fish, I thought it might have been one of the giant catfish that I knew inhabited the lake. As I got closer, though, I could see the scales of a carp just beneath the surface, and after some gentle probing with the net handle, the line came free and I was in direct contact again. At that point, the water exploded as the carp surged off into open water where I was able, eventually, to play and net the fish. I made my way back to shore with my prize.

I paused for breath and peered down into my net. A huge common! We rested, the carp and myself, in the margins while we regained our composure somewhat. Then, leaving the fish in the net, I climbed back on the bank. I asked a passer-by if they would take a photo. As I struggled with the net, I realised I might have something a bit special. On the scales it went: 34lb! A fit, superbly conditioned fish. After the photos, I put the carp back in the net and waded back out into the margins to release her. Lowering one side of the net, I eased the carp's head gently forward, cradling it in the water until it got its bearings. Then, with a kick of its tail, it was gone.

CHAPTER FOURTEEN

Tench

Quest For A 'Double'

Perspective.

On my local carp syndicate's water one hot summer after-noon, I'd arrived only to find the carp heavily involved in spawning at the causeway end of the lake. Against a long row of sedges, most of the carp population could be seen crashing, rolling and generally having fun. Luckily I hadn't lugged all my gear the third of a mile or so from the car park. Instead, I had just brought along a bait bucket to stake my claim to any swim that took my fancy. Most responsible anglers don't fish for spawning carp, the theory being that they will be uninterested in feeding during the event, and stressed and exhausted after it. So carp fishing was out for the time being. The lake, however, held some good tench and a few big bream, remnants of a once large shoal. I thought it might be a good opportunity to have a go for these.

I continued my walk round the pit, stopping momentarily at a swim called 'No Carp'. As I gazed out looking for signs of life, a large fish rolled about 20 yards straight in front of the peg. I put my bucket down and hotfooted it back to the car to fetch my tackle, pretty sure that what I'd seen was a big tench or bream. I always keep a cross-section of gear in the car and, as well as the big carp rods, I had a couple of Wilson Avons, really great rods in my opinion. Two mini baitrunners matched them nicely, loaded with 8lb sensor line. I grabbed a few other bits. A bivvy wasn't needed as I didn't intend to stay the night. Suitably equipped, I hurried back to 'No Carp'. (Why does every lake have a swim called 'No Carp?')

On arriving back, I rigged up. Attaching a small Arlesey Bomb, I cast as gently as I could to where I had seen the fish roll. The bottom was fairly clear except for a light covering of silkweed. With this in mind, I tied on 2 feet of 6lb fluorocarbon line as a hook link. Two grains of corn were impaled on a size 12 hook and a split shot placed up the line. The small bomb sat above to create a simple running leger set-up. I hoped the whole rig would sit nicely on top of the weed and the bright yellow corn seen by the fish. I catapulted out some loose grains, placed the rod on a buzzer and sat back.

The afternoon was muggy, with very little wind. Out in the lake there was another almighty swirl and this time I saw quite clearly the dorsal fin of a big bream. I had caught them before, up to 10lb, while carp fishing from the lake. Although very impressive creatures, winching a bream in on carp tackle at three in the morning is not really 'cricket'. Here was an opportunity to fish for them with appropriate tackle and in daylight, which for any specimen fish is unusual, but for big bream especially so. A unique set of circumstances, though probably most diehard carpers would have gone down the pub or done almost anything else but fish deliberately for bream.

One hour passed, then two. I dozed. Suddenly the buzzer let out a half-dozen bleeps. I was only using one rod, and as I came to my senses I noticed the line had moved about eight feet from where I had cast it. I picked up the rod and swept it back in a slightly over-enthusiastic strike into . . . thin air. A line bite most probably. Fully alert now, I rebaited and cast out again. Five minutes passed, and then the bobbin rose steadily to the butt. I struck again, this time into solid resistance.

The Wilson Avon took on a pleasing curve and battle was joined. A few minutes later a big slab slid into the landing net. On the scales it weighed 12lb 2oz. A new personal best! I was delighted.

On the opposite bank, another syndicate member, Terry Greening, had turned up with his son Brad. I could see they were debating whether to fish or not. Those in the know will have heard of the Greenings, fine anglers all, with Brad and Rob going on to become well known on the carp-fishing scene. At this point, Brad would have been 12 or 13 and Terry, noticing the commotion in my swim, had dispatched Brad with a camera to take some snaps. I rested the fish in the margins until it got its bearings and paused for reflection. I thought of myself as a 12-year-old, fishing the Pits at Stanstead Abbotts. My dream was to catch a 2½lb bream. A proper fish, in my dad's opinion. I used to hang on his every word as he would recount (every time we went fishing) the story of the capture of his personal best bream, a whopping 5lb! Bradley arrived with the camera.

'Had one then?' he enquired.

'Yes,' I beamed. 'Bream, twelve pounds, two ounces.'

'Oh,' he said.

I lifted the fish from the mat. It was a magnificent specimen. Deep-bodied, pigeon-chested with jet black fins. As Brad snapped away he casually mentioned that his personal-best bream was over 13lb. My smile decreased somewhat. Then again, he'd already caught carp to 30lb and tench to over 12lb, so to this 13-year-old a 12lb bream wasn't such a big deal.

That's what I mean about perspective.

That event illustrated to me how fishing and fish sizes have changed over the years. As I got back into fishing in the 1990s, I started buying the weekly magazines *Angler's Mail* and *Angling Times*. With the abolition of the old close season on still waters in 1996, more reports of exceptionally large fish started appearing in the press, double-figure tench especially. With my personal best at the time a modest 4½lb, I resolved at some point to try and improve on that.

I was also developing a different perspective in other areas of my life, and the beginning of the nineties brought big changes. Two years after the arrival of our son Dylan in 1989, our twins Natasha and Brittany were born. Identical and adorable, they resisted my efforts to get them to take up fishing, and still do now. Where did I go wrong?

Apart from rediscovering my love for fishing, I'd also started playing football again. Watching the Italia 1990 World Cup had been really exciting, so, suitably inspired, I joined a local side – the Chalfont Wasps. I was becoming more active on the music front, and my brother-in-law, Carl Dufresne, had come over from Canada to stay with us for a while. Carl is a musician too, so of course we starting jamming and going through some songs I had been working on with Maiden. We then decided it might be fun to get a band together, with the intention of playing covers and a few originals. I drafted in ex-bassist for The Cult, Jamie Stewart, who I'd already been writing with, and drummer Ray Weston. This line-up was to become the basis of The Untouchables, and we gigged on and off for the next couple of years. I was a bit wary at first, unsure if I really wanted to get back into full-time touring and recording. I was happy to be playing and singing again, and doing the rounds of the club circuit really helped me regain my self-confidence.

So, with work commitments, a wife and three young children, I didn't really turn my attention to tench until around 2008. I'd read some reports about tench in the small lake at Wellington Country Park in Berkshire. In those days I used to drop my son Dylan off at school in Henley on Monday mornings, so one Sunday evening saw me stashing some tackle in the boot of the car, intending to drop in at the lake on the way back from the school run.

Wellington was a very productive tench fishery and I landed a couple of sixes on my first trip, easily beating my old personal best. There was also a lake called Tolpits, run by the Watford Piscators angling club, close to my home. Well known for its large carp up to 50lb, it also held a good head of tench, including a few doubles.

The spring of 2008 saw me conduct my first real tench campaign. I normally fished for two or three days. Arriving in the late afternoon, I'd bait up, fish up until dark, then wind in, putting some more bait out before retiring to the tent to get some sleep. Up again at first light, I'd fill the feeders and get the rods out onto the spot, and then top up with a few balls of groundbait laced with casters, hemp and so on. The action usually wouldn't be too long in coming, and fishing between dawn and lunchtime, half-a-dozen tench would normally be landed. Average size seemed to be around 6lb. I also caught bream just into double figures and the odd roach to over a pound.

Great fun on light feeder gear. In fact, I really started to enjoy this type of fishing; re-casting, knocking up groundbait and hitting runs really added up to an enjoyable, active session. I think even the most ardent carp anglers would admit to getting bored sat in a bivvy for days on end waiting for a big fish to make a mistake. I've done my fair share of that myself. I found tench fishing a nice change from hunting carp. The seeds of an obsession were sown.

Enjoyable though those early 'tenching' sessions were, it was clear I'd have to move on if I wanted to catch bigger fish. Maiden always geared up for touring during spring, which was generally accepted as the best time for big tench. Rehearsals usually took place in May in readiness for either the European festival season or a summer swing through America. Looking at the touring schedule for 2008 to 2009 though, I spotted a window of opportunity. The *Somewhere Back in Time* tour would be our most ambitious yet. The plan was, as well as a full European and US tour, to visit places we hadn't played for a while, including Australia. The problem with touring the southern hemisphere is cost. In other words, by the time you have transported the whole crew, band and equipment all that way, the cost involved outweighs the income. Simple logistics.

Bruce Dickinson's passion for flying is well known and he came up with the idea of kitting out a Boeing 757 for touring. The fact that this plane would take all our equipment plus band and crew would make it cost effective. Even better was that the tour would run from February 2008 to April 2009. This would mean I would have April and May 2009 to concentrate on fishing for tench. Very good management, I think.

The 757 would be the ultimate in band transport. I had to laugh when I thought back to my first band Urchin and the different forms of transport we used in those formative years. The first van we owned was an old Bowyers meat wagon! Despite painting it a disgusting brown colour, we couldn't quite cover up the Bowyers logo on the side of the van which featured a six-foot high cross-section of a pork pie. The interior of the vehicle also never quite lost the fragrance of slightly out of date sausages. It was comfortable enough inside though. 'Big' Dave Lewis, our roadie, was older than us and quite handy with a toolbox. He had partitioned the back half of the jalopy to house the equipment, and built two benches running sideways along the walls of the van in the front for the band to sit on. This worked fine until whoever was driving (usually Dave) took a corner a bit too enthusiastically and we'd all end up in a heap on the floor. I have to say I owe a great deal to Dave, who sadly is no longer with us. He really believed in Urchin and was a real driving force behind the band. I don't think I would have got to where I am now without his help: so, thanks, 'Big' Dave – wherever you are.

My venue for spring 2009 was to be my local carp syndicate's water, where I had caught that large bream. Reports had been filtering out of carp anglers catching lots of tench, leading to much mickey taking among the members, of course.

Full of anticipation, I pulled into the car park of the fishery on a pleasant spring afternoon. I noticed another chap unloading his kit so I wandered over for a chat. The man in question turned out to be a well-known carp angler and one of the guys who had recently been plagued by tench. After the usual pleasantries were exchanged, I asked him about his recent tench exploits.

'Yeah, bleeding fings,' he said. 'I caught about fifteen of 'em.'

Music to my ears. I mentioned I was going to have a go for them and, before I could press him any further, he told me the exact spot he had been fishing, a swim called the Mirror. Even better news was that ever since word got out that it had been producing lots of tench, the members had been avoiding it like the plague so it would more than likely be free. The stars were aligning.

The swim was indeed free. I'd fished it before while carping, and its main feature was a lovely smooth, firm, clay-bottomed strip about 20 yards straight out. I decided to fish my two rods on this spot. Tactics would be in-line large maggot feeders tied to an 8lb fluorocarbon hook length with a size 12 Drennan barbel hook, and two buoyant rubber maggots mounted on a hair. The mainline was 10lb sensor, and my mini Shimano 5000 baitrunners were matched with two Wychwood 1¾lb barbel rods.

With the day wearing on I set up camp, intending to spend the next two days and nights there. I spodded a couple of pints of hemp and maggots on to the spot, and catapulted out a dozen balls of groundbait to get some scent in the water. Apart from a tench of around 5lb just before dusk, the evening was uneventful. I was pretty sure the tench would be active in the morning. I wound the rods in for the night, and then put a few more spodfuls of bait out before getting into my sleeping bag.

I was up at first light the next morning. I put the kettle on, then filled up the feeders and whacked them out, already clipped up, onto the spot. I then sent several balls of groundbait crashing through the mirror-calm surface, a violent contrast to the serenity of the dawn. I sat back and surveyed the scene. Mist clung to the glassy surface of the lake, and at the far end of the pit a carp flung itself clear of the water and landed with a tremendous crash. Out in the middle of the lake in front of me, another fish rolled. The first show was subtle, a black fin and its back cut noiselessly through the oily surface film. Tench maybe? I trained my eyes on the same spot.

Five minutes later and a bit closer to me: slap! Definitely a tench this time, the characteristic tail slap giving the game away. So it continued for the next 30 minutes or so, the showing fish moving closer to me, with the last sighting just beyond my baited patch. Then all was quiet.

I could just imagine a shoal of tench moving onto the bed of bait I had put down. These are the moments you live for as an angler: when the scenario you have had in your head so many times crystallises into reality. Rare perfection.

Bleep! The squeal of the alarm split the morning calm. Tench on! After a lively scrap I netted a good fish. On the scales it went: 7lb 4oz. A new personal best! I had only just returned the fish when the other rod was away: 6lb 4oz for this one. And so it continued for the rest of the morning. In all, I landed eight fish, including two sevens and the rest all over 6lb. I wound in around lunchtime and retired to my bivvy for a much-needed sleep. The rest of the session passed relatively uneventfully, with only a couple of fives gracing my net the next morning. I was more than happy with my haul, though, and couldn't wait to get back for another session.

It was mid-May before I managed to clear some time for a 24-hour trip to the lake. I arrived in the early evening on Wednesday and set up shop. I repeated the usual routine of baiting up and letting the swim rest for the night, ready for a dawn start the next day. Luckily I managed to bag the same swim so I was confident of some action. Little did I know, I was about to have the session of a lifetime.

Up at dawn, I saw that the tench were active as usual. They were rolling out in the middle of the pit and I assumed it would be only a matter of time before a *Tinca tinca* graced my net. No bites were forthcoming, though. I had tackled up with my usual 1¾lb rods and maggot feeders. I was just think-ing about a change of tactics when the right-hand rod abso-lutely tore off. I grabbed the rod and knew straightaway by the savage power and strength on the other end that it was a carp, and a good one by the feel of it. I had faith in my set-up, though. I thought it well balanced. Put it this way, if you attached the hook to a fence post and bent the rod at full compression, you would have a job to snap the line. Add to that the swim was completely free of snags (I had fished it many times), and I thought landing a carp would be no problem. The carp had other ideas.

After battling to and fro for about five minutes, all went quiet. I was a bit mystified, as the fish was in open water with no visible obstacles to cause trouble. I could only imagine the fish had found an old piece of machinery, a pipe or something, left over from when the pit was dug. I eventually managed to retrieve the rig, minus the fish. On winding in, I was greeted by a sorry sight. The big Drennan feeder was mangled, with half of it missing; the line was frayed and the hook link had parted midway down. Time for a rethink.

I still had my carp rods in the car, so I wound in my other rod and went to fetch them. Back in the swim, I rigged up the 2¾lb ESP Terry Hearn carp rods fitted with Daiwa Infinity reels loaded with 12lb line. I changed the hook link to 10lb Gardner coated braid, and opted for 2oz in-line leads and PVA stockings filled with maggots. Two rubber grubs would be hair-rigged on a size 10 Drennan barbel hook. Not ideal for the tench, but after the experience earlier I was taking no chances.

Half an hour later I had another run. This time a stuttering-type take. Connecting with the fish, resistance was minimal. Bream! At 10lb 2oz, it was a pretty sorry-looking male covered in spawning tubercles. Still, a double-figure bream was still a special fish in my book. This catch prompted me to change tactics again. Back out with the lighter rods, this time beefed up with the 10lb hook links. I thought this set-up now would be a good all-round solution. And so it proved to be.

The fishing fantasy film I had run many times in my head played out in a full-blown epic that morning. This was its cast of characters in order of appearance:

8am: 10lb 2oz bream

9am: 26lb 8oz common carp

10.30am: 12lb mirror carp

11am: 13lb 6oz bream (new personal best)

12pm: 8lb tench

A pretty amazing session. The 13lb 6oz bream was a fine specimen, in contrast to the sorry-looking male I had earlier. It reminded me of one of those 1950s cartoon seaside postcards where the female of the species is large, fat and dominant of her scrawny male counterpart. No doubt she'd give him 'what for' when they were reunited.

With the sun now well up and the temperature heading into the 70s, I re-cast the rods. I needed to catch up on some sleep but before doing so I rigged up a maggot clip on one rod. This was a new gadget where you could load maggots onto a clip that was attached to your hair rig. Basically, it's a Medusa rig without the hassle. I crammed as many grubs as I could onto the clip and attached a big PVA stocking full of maggots to the size 10. I cast the rig out onto the baited spot and collapsed on to my bed-chair and almost instantly fell into a deep sleep. I don't usually like sleeping when fishing as the fishing part of my brain won't let me sleep properly and the part that wants to sleep prevents me from angling effectively. Thank God for bite alarms on this occasion, though. I was wrenched from my dreams by an absolute 'one toner' on my left-hand rod. The maggot clip rod had torn off.

I wriggled out of the sleeping bag and scrambled to the rods with the alarm still whining. Pulling into the fish, I thought it was probably another carp, such was its power, but I dared to hope I was playing a double-figure tench at last. The fish fought hard and deep, but I was winning. I brought the fish carefully to the margins, and as it turned over a few feet below I could see it was a tench. A big one too. It was beaten now, and I netted it first time. A closer look revealed a fish in a different class to anything I'd seen before. Not a double, but a perfectly proportioned fish of 8lb and another personal best. That, as they say, was the icing on the cake on what was one of the best sessions ever.

The next year or two was taken up with lots of touring. I also bought a house on America's West Coast, so I was spending less and less time in the UK. On the music front I was busy, returning to Compass Point Studios in Nassau, Bahamas, in January 2010 to record what was to become Maiden's *The Final Frontier* album. Before going to Nassau, we set up camp in Paris to finish writing and rehearsing some of the new songs. I prepared well for the album, and had been holed up in my home studio for a couple of weeks before travelling to France. I had around 12 new song ideas that I'd be taking to Paris with me. I had a vague idea about pursuing more of a progressive direction on the album, and a few of the songs we ended up doing, such as 'Starblind' and 'Isle of Avalon', featured a few quirky time signatures.

One morning in Paris I decided to go and have a few hours fishing in a local park lake. Before leaving the hotel, I saw bassist and bandleader Steve Harris and dropped off a tape on which I had recorded an idea I had. He told me he would have a listen and get back to me in a few days to let me know what he thought.

Two hours later, I'd just got my second rod out when my mobile phone rang. It was Steve. He was enthusing about the tape I'd given him, saying he had written most of the words already and it had given him an idea for a concept and artwork for the album. The song turned out to be the title track 'The Final Frontier', and it would be the opening song on the album, coming in after the overture of 'Satellite 15'.

This double whammy would also provide a dramatic opening to our new live show when we toured the album the following summer. I was really chuffed that the idea I had given him had sparked such inspiration. I also hoped I didn't get a belting run from a carp in the middle of our excited conversation.

I'd also taken time out that year to sort out a long-standing medical problem. For the past three years, I'd been hobbling around with a partially torn Achilles tendon in my left leg, and now the cortisone and steroid injections that had kept me going were having little effect. On the last American tour, I had been jumping about on stage using just one leg, and even walking for

more than ten minutes was impossible. It was time for an operation. After consulting several different surgeons, I decided to go
with Dr Simon Moyes, who I'm glad to say did a great job, with
my Achilles now as good as new.

The first leg of *The Final Frontier* tour took us through the
USA and Canada before another month of dates, finishing off in
Valencia, Spain. It was the beginning of September 2010 when I
found myself back in the UK again. I didn't really have a tench
water in mind at the time. Then glancing through the match
reports of a local club's website, I saw that a lake quite close to
me was producing the odd large tench. I had fished the lake in
Wraysbury back in the 1990s, and although I saw lots of tench, I
had failed to catch any. It was a pretty lake of about seven acres.
The only minus point was that it was noisy, being located right
next to a busy junction on the M25 motorway. Still, it held the
stamp of fish I was after, with the tench reported in the club
match weighing over 9lb. I purchased a club book and looked
forward to my return trip.

I arrived at the lake one weekday afternoon. Although there
was a drivable path around most of the lake, I elected to park up
and walk. I donned Polaroid sunglasses and, carrying a marker
float rod, set off for a recce. The main feature was easily visible,
a gravel bar that ran the full length of the pit. On one side, near
the busy road, the margins were deep, 10 to 12 feet. On the other
side of the bar, the quieter willow side, the silty lake bed shelved
gently, bottoming out at around 6 feet. Also at the end of the pit
was a small island about the size of a 3-ton truck.

I decided to concentrate on the willow side of the lake. I thought with it still being so warm the fish would be favouring the shallower water. It was also a lot quieter over that side and a bit more pleasant to fish. Night fishing and camping on the lake were not allowed, so most of my sessions were afternoon into dusk. But if I was pursuing tench, shouldn't I have been at the water at daybreak? Yes, well maybe, though I think early mornings would be OK if they started a little later . . .

I caught well pretty much from the start. Bream, good ones, too, up to 8lb, and carp, loads of them, mostly in the 3 or 4lb bracket. On speaking to the bailiff one day he informed me, voice raised over the constant roar of the traffic, that the controlling club had stocked a thousand of the little blighters a few months earlier. Ah, that would explain why I wasn't getting through to the tench. Still, I persevered. I knew for a fact there were a few big tench in there but perhaps a different strategy was needed to pick up one out from the hordes of small carp. My thoughts turned back to the small island at the end of the lake. Although on the noisy side, I did fancy the peg and decided to check it out. A feel around with my marker rod revealed a nice hard bottom in about ten feet of water where the island shelved away sharply, then levelled out. I decided to bait this area and not fish it for a week or two, thinking bigger carp and hopefully the tench would bully the smaller fish out the area.

I peppered the swim with large pellets, 18ml halibut boilies and hemp for the next couple of weeks. One good thing about the night-fishing ban was that the lake was usually quiet during the week. This, and the fact it was only a 15-minute drive from my house, meant I could visit regularly to fish or just bait up.

September drifted into October and the nights started drawing in. Long pants and a fleece replaced shorts and flip-flops as my fishing garb. I fished my baited island area three or four times and, though I'd landed carp nudging 20lb and some good bream, still no tench. But I was sure if I kept at it I'd get that big *Tinca*. After all, 'he who walks in the eightfold noble path with unswerving determination is sure to reach Nirvana,' as they (or at least Buddha) say. And it was not as if I was suffering. I was really enjoying my short sessions on the pit. I was fishing method feeders at this point, with small halibut boilies tipped with corn and a halibut method mix. Rods were the usual Wychwoods with mini baitrunners and a 10lb line. I could drive right to the peg as well. Add to that the fact I had the place pretty much to myself, an evening session would always produce two or three bites. As soon as a fish was hooked my first reaction was always the same. Could it be a tench? And then it happened.

By now it was late October and I decided to have one last crack at the lake before the weather turned too cold. I arrived at the swim mid-afternoon, as usual, planning to fish to just into dark. A cold wind blew down the pit, dislodging the odd leaf from the bankside birch trees. I cast out both rods, then set up the brolly to keep the wind off. I put the kettle on, slid gratefully into my thermal suit and hunkered down to await events. The afternoon passed into evening and eventually the witching hour: that fleeting period between day and night. I have lost count of how many good fish I've landed at dusk, my favourite time of the fishing day.

I had been getting most of my bites from the right-hand side of the swim for some reason. Maybe it was where the fish entered the area on their patrol route. Anyway, it was the right-hand rod that registered a bite and I was straight on it, line singing in the wind, playing a heavy fish. Could it be? The fish stayed deep all the way to the margins as I kept pressure on it. It was almost dark now as the fish was drawn towards the landing net. My head-torch revealed all. A tench, and a big one!

In a bit of a flap I set up the scales sling and camera: 9lb 1oz! My biggest yet. I was ecstatic. It was a long fish that looked as though it could go into double figures at the right time of year. With no one else at the lake, I did a few self-take photos, and then returned the big *Tinca* back to her home.

CHAPTER FIFTEEN

Jumbo Jets And Jumbo Tench

The next few years featured a lot of touring and we took out the big plane again to complete the second leg of the *Final Frontier* tour. Just to clear up speculation, we don't own our own 757 jumbo jet. We rent it, fit it out for our needs and, when we're done, it reverts to being just another passenger plane. Albeit one with the band's name in 15-foot-high lettering on the fuselage. Oh, and a giant emaciated skull emblazoned on the tail.

I've had mixed feelings over the years about the whole Eddie mascot thing. When I first joined the band, being young and idealistic I thought Eddie was a bit of a distraction, unnecessary even. All the bands I grew up listening to, like Free, Humble Pie and Deep Purple, didn't have gimmicks as such. But that was in the 1970s. Bands just got up there in jeans and T-shirts, turned up their amps loud and played. But when you think about it, that was a gimmick in itself. It was all new, different and exciting. By the late 1970s that had become the norm. I suppose it became harder to stand out from the crowd. Eddie certainly stood out, and in the early touring days the money made from merchandising certainly helped to keep the band afloat. This enabled us to stay on the road, taking the music to the fans all over the world. Eddie works on so many levels. He can be completely outrageous, leaving us band members to 'keep it real' and be ourselves. Not try to be celebrities.

When not on the road I had got back into carp fishing, and it wasn't until around 2015 that I turned my attention to tench again. Between 2015 and 2017 I tried a number of different waters to catch that elusive double. Probably the best known of these was Mid Kent Fisheries's Milton Pan lake in Kent. This was where Martin Bowler filmed his *Catching the Impossible* tench episode of 2009. In the sequence, he lands a stonking double-figured tench as well as a rake of others during the session. In fact, for a while Milton Pan was probably the best big tench water in the country.

Sadly, by the time I got to fish it the stocks of big tench were in decline and most if not all of the doubles had died off. Just the work of nature, the fish being old. I didn't even see a tench roll in the half-dozen 48-hour sessions I did there. I did catch a bull-dozer of a common carp, though, at 28lb, and also photographed a 15lb 8oz bream for another member.

Devils Lane Lake in Surrey was reported to hold doubles, but I never really got to grips with it. I didn't feel comfortable night fishing there so did days only. I worked at it, building my own swims, raking out huge piles of weed and baiting up regularly. No tench were caught or even seen. I did manage a few low double-figure carp, though.

Then there was the Sheep Walk complex in Shepperton, Surrey. The big lake still holds the record for tench, a spawn-laden fish of 15lb 3oz. After spotting some very big tench in the adjacent lake, Little Sheep Walk, I decided to have a go on there. Once again, it proved difficult. Night fishing was uncomfortable, with the fishery being open to all and sundry. I did stick it out on a few occasions. I also rarely saw fish showing. They were there, though. Once I went down for an evening dark-float fishing session. At around 8pm the tench started to roll all over the lake and continued until dusk. You would have thought that the lake was absolutely stuffed with them. Big fish too, their huge tails slapping the water, probably feeding on a hatch of insects. Tench on a fly? I think on this occasion, maybe. Certainly my corn was ignored.

I even bit the bullet and did a few sessions on the very busy Linear Fisheries in Oxford. Nothing. Suffolk Water Park for a few nights? Nada. The 40-acre North Troy lake near my home? Zilch.

Another venue on my radar was Korda Lake in the Colne Valley near Harefield. Run by the British Carp Study Group it was not only a fine carp water but also held big tench up to 14lb as well as quite a few other doubles. It was also five minutes from my front door. I knew one of the members of the BCSG, Gary Newman, through a mutual friend. I would bump into Gary from time to time, and talk fishing of course. I knew he loved his tench fishing and I would drop hints about Korda, hoping that he would pick up on it but he never did. Then one day, when I bumped into him in Harefield tackle shop, I just flat-out asked him. What were the chances of a Korda ticket? No problem, he said, I just had to fill out the form and he would 'second' me. This was great news. Access to a specimen tench water on my doorstep!

I would have to bide my time. The band would start *The Book of Souls* tour in February 2016, and it would run right through until August. This would include places we'd never played before, like China and El Salvador. Playing in El Salvador was a bit of an eye-opener. We took out an even bigger jumbo jet specially fitted out for band, crew and gear. With the band's name and logo plastered all over the plane, we couldn't go anywhere unnoticed. This was not the band's idea, I can assure you. We would just as soon creep about anonymously when we're not on stage. No, this was a master stroke of marketing on our managers' part! The upshot was that wherever we landed the plane, especially in places such as South America, there would be TV news crews waiting and crowds gathered inside and outside the airport. Getting from the plane to our transport could be a nightmare with all the airport staff, customs people and even, on one occasion, the flight controllers wanting selfies and autographs. Begging the question, who was keeping an eye on all the planes? After getting bundled into waiting cars, we would then speed off to the hotel, fans following us in convoy, honking and cheering, and news helicopters filming everything from above. Madness!

El Salvador, with its recent bloody history – including a 13-year civil war that ended in 1992 – left a lasting impression. I looked out of my hotel room window when we first arrived and saw around 200 fans. Half an hour later, the fans were gone, replaced with 50 or so heavily armed riot police. The show was fantastic, though, with a really passionate response from the kids in the audience. You could really feel them letting off steam, and I didn't blame them. No doubt life was hard for some people there, and simple pleasures like music and football, wherever you are, can help numb the pain of the tough facts of life. We even got a thank-you from the government for coming to play in El Salvador, as not many bands bother. They hoped that the fact the show (the biggest in the country's history, with 25,000 fans in attendance) went off without any trouble would demonstrate that the country was safer than it used to be.

A few weeks later, I was chilling out by the pool on a day off in Santiago, Chile, when Collie – John Collins, one of our tour managers – strolled over and casually informed me that Ed Force One, our plane, had been in an accident at the airport. A collision with a tow truck had badly damaged the engine. Fortunately, no one was seriously injured, but it meant that the aircraft was out of action for a while. Amazingly, our team managed to get the gear, band and crew to the next show 700 miles away in Córdoba, Argentina, the very next night. Meanwhile, a team of aircraft specialists were flown out from Finland to repair the damage to Ed Force One and, incredibly, only 11 days after the accident they flew the plane down to re-join the tour in Brazil. The repair crew were brought backstage before the show as we wanted to thank them personally. I was expecting them to be studious boffin types but the six staggering Icelanders that came into the dressing room were anything but. I have seldom seen men so drunk, yet still remain standing.

'Hallooow, niche to meech yoo,' slurred one fella, staggering forward under the sheer weight of alcohol.

Of course, these guys had been working around the clock for the last ten days and nights. They were just letting off a bit of steam, which was fair enough. I just hope they had tightened up all the nuts and bolts.

The rest of the tour went smoothly and, after a swing through Europe finishing off at the 2016 Wacken Festival, I was finally back in the UK and itching to have a crack at Korda Lake. It was now early August as I pulled through the gates of the fishery on a blisteringly hot day. I didn't plan to fish on this occasion, but had instead just brought a plumbing rod and some bait. The lake has numerous features. As well as the gravel bars there are plateaus, gullies and, now in midsummer, big beds of thick weed. Also, the pit had a lot of signal crayfish, so in all a little tricky. If I were to have any success, I knew I'd have to put in the time to gather as much knowledge as possible. In the first few weeks I got to know some of the regulars. The guys who fished the lake were refreshingly old school: good anglers who had caught their share of big fish and were happy to pass on information.

I did two or three of these recce trips before I did any fishing, so I was full of anticipation as I bumped my way around the rough road that circles the lake for my first proper session. I was heading for a swim called the Ants. The peg had been producing the odd fish while the rest of the lake had been in the usual midsummer doldrums. I thought it would be a good place to start. There was a three-rod rule on Korda. I don't usually like fishing with three rods, but as the lake was fishing quite hard, I thought it would give me more of a chance. I decided to go with mini Tiger Nut boilies on two rods and plastic corn on the other. I found a nice clear area of firm silt about 60 yards out, in 8 feet of water, so the middle rod went there along with some Spomb boilies, corn, hemp and particles. The right-hand rod was fished up against a gravel bar and the area was baited.

The left-hand side of the swim offered a multiple-choice of features and I eventually decided to concentrate on a gravel plateau around 40 yards out, in 5 feet of water. It was bordering on hard work getting all three rods out, working under the full glare of the August sun now beginning to descend in the west directly opposite me. I was happy with the position of the baits, though, and it was worth the effort to get them all fishing effectively – especially as I was going to be there for the next 72 hours.

The rest of the day passed uneventfully. At around 7pm I pan-fried a fillet steak and poured myself a glass of wine. As the evening wore on, I sat looking out across the lake for signs of fish. At that moment, there was no place I'd rather be.

I didn't see anything show and the lake seemed almost devoid of life, save for the odd coot chattering in the distance. I usually wind in the rods at night, but on this occasion decided to leave them out. It was still and muggy, and I slept fitfully, the odd bleep from the bite indicators getting me raised up on one elbow to look out at the rods. Crayfish probably, I thought. I wasn't too worried. I'd hardened up some of the boilies to use as hookbait by leaving them on the dashboard of my car in the hot sun for the last couple of days.

At about 2am, the middle Delkim let out a few bleeps then signalled a 'one toner'. I was in! I scrambled out of the sleeping bag and bent into the fish. After a lively scrap, I landed a mirror carp around mid-double figures. I took a few shots of the fish on the mat, then released it back into the pit, well pleased with my early success.

Nothing happened for the rest of the night and it wasn't until just after dawn that I had some more action. This time the signal came from the right-hand rod, fished tight up against a gravel bar running out to the lake. I pulled into the fish, and a few minutes later a 6lb tench was posing for the camera.

The next 36 hours passed, but no more fish came to the net. I packed up, happy with my first two fish from this tricky lake.

I was back a few days later. I had my eye on a swim that had not received much attention. I thought with the lake getting quite a bit of pressure, the fish might be attracted to this area that had not been fished for a while. Also, there were some good features and, with the line lay being slightly different, this increased my confidence. Such an important factor in fishing.

By now I was using Mainline pineapple pop-ups on all three rods. Tied on a size 8 or 10 Mugga hook to a Gardner 10lb Speciskin silt-coloured hook length, the little boilies sat up nicely just above any detritus on the bottom, masking the hook in the process. The skin was peeled a half inch from the eye of the hook, giving only a slight hinge effect. I wanted to keep the hook link fairly stiff, as the resident crayfish could make a real mess of anything too supple. Leads were inline 2oz flat jobs fished bolt-rig style. I didn't use any lead core as the 12lb fluorocarbon mainline I was using would ensure the end tackle was kept on the deck. As an aid to this, I pinched on a few blobs of heavy putty at intervals up the line above the end tackle. I had also bought myself a couple of new Drennan Distance 2lb TC rods.

I had arrived at the fishery around midday on Wednesday and, after a quick catch-up with a few of the regulars, made my way around to the swim known as the Royal Box.

It was a little overgrown, but with a bit of work with some secateurs I had in the car, I got the peg fishable. I stood hands on hips surveying my handiwork, sweating in the still hot late-afternoon sun. I didn't know it then, but this was going to turn out to be a great session.

With the swim cleared I set to work with the Spomb rod, and made up some groundbait. My plan was to bait up heavily at first, then top the spots up as needed with a few pouchfuls of the mini boilies and egg-sized balls of groundbait. This, I thought, would keep any fish in the area mooching around, without disturbing the swim too much. By the time I finished baiting, setting up the bivvy and cooking an evening meal, it was around 10pm. I decided not to fish that night and get some sleep before getting up for a dawn start.

I was up bright and early, and soon had the rods out and fishing. I sat back enjoying the stillness of the early morning with a freshly made cup of tea. Peering into the margins of my swim, I could see the odd crayfish scuttling back and forth. I dropped a couple of broken boilies into the water, expecting the crayfish to attack them immediately, but they remained untouched. The scent of watermint hung heavily in the damp morning air, and on the far bank I saw another angler emerge slowly from his bivvy. The morning turned into afternoon and then evening with no action to my rods.

I turned in early that night after topping up the spots with a bit more bait. This time, I decided to leave the rods out fishing for the night. OK, I was getting desperate. No bites disturbed my sleep, though, and I was up again at first light, sitting by the rods. As the light grew I could make out the old patch of bubbles appearing over my right-hand rod. These were the creamy, fishy sort that stay on the surface for a long while as opposed to the gassy type that come up and pop almost immediately.

Suddenly, the right-hand rod burst into life. I found myself playing a heavy fish. In the growing light, I could see the line cutting through the water as the fish powered out into the pit. *No tench this*, I thought, *it feels much too heavy*. A few minutes later I drew a big carp over the landing net. Resting the fish, I set about the ritual of organising the scales and mat, and set up the camera for some self-takes. With everything ready, I squatted down, grabbed the net and attempted to lift the fish from water. At that moment, I realised that I had something a bit special. On the mat, the fish looked huge, and on the scales it was 40lb 4oz. A real old character of a mirror carp, and one of the lake's originals.

After getting a few shots, I returned the carp and got the rod back out on the spot. I catapulted out 20 or so boilies and sat back with a big smile on my face. Half an hour later, I was in again on the same rod. This time a common of 17lb took a liking to the little yellow pop-up. The right-hand side of the swim was rocking now with big patches of bubbles and fish crashing at intervals, looking like they were hard on the feed. I was able to top up the swim by putting out boilies in ones and twos, and I thought this might be giving me a little edge as opposed to crashing a Spomb of bait right on top of the fish.

An hour later, a stuttering take on the same rod saw me on my feet and bent into another fish. Not quite the savage power this time, but the jagging fight told me this could be a big tench. After a few runs and tail slaps in the margins, I slipped the net under a mottled fish of 8lb. That signalled the end of the action for the day. No double-figure tench yet, but what a session!

Just then, an angler I had seen on the far bank popped into my swim. 'Pash', a long-time angler on the lake, had seen me landing the fish and was curious. I showed him some shots of the big carp, and he confirmed it was one of the original stock, a fish known as Cluster. He congratulated me and, after a chat, he went off looking for a new swim.

I decided then to catch up on some rest, but the day was hot and sleep was difficult in the stifling confines of the bivvy. I baited the swim again at around 4pm, and an hour later an angler moved into the swim next to me to my left, followed a little while later by another immediately to my right. Although there was a fair distance between us, I thought that all those lines cutting through the water would upset the fish. And so it proved, as the rest of the session resulted in just one lost fish. I was happy with my three-fish tally, though, when I packed up.

I fished the lake hard for the rest of the summer and into late autumn. I really enjoyed the fishing, and by keeping in touch with what was going on at the lake and fishing it regularly, I notched up 14 fish comprised of seven carp and seven tench.

The next nine months were taken up pursuing other species and, of course, more travelling. *The Book of Souls* tour kicked off its second leg in Antwerp in April 2017, and was to include our biggest British tour for some time before coming to an end in late July after a swing through North America. In Leeds, well-known carper and rock fan Julian Cundiff came to the show. We met backstage around 15 minutes before showtime, me standing there in my 'stage gear' and Julian preaching the gospel of sharpened hooks, after which he presented me with a packet of them. Tucked in my back pocket, they remained there for the whole show.

It wasn't until spring 2019 that my thoughts turned once again to tench. Finding myself with a week to kill in France, I decided on a slightly mad whim to investigate the Lake of the Orient. I say mad because the lake when at full capacity is almost 6,000 acres. This vast water has become a Mecca for carp fishermen over the last few decades. The anglers are attracted by the possibility of catching a really special fish. But with the stakes set so high, it is not an easy game. Weeks can go by without a bite, and the lake can change from flat calm to an angry cauldron of whitecaps in minutes.

I'd read a few articles on the Orient. I was particularly interested in carp angler Darrell Peck's series of articles in the magazine *Carpworld*. In these he recounted not only captures of big carp, but huge tench. I managed to get in touch with Darrell through a friend, Christian Olde Wolbers (who happens to be the ex-bass player for the band Fear Factory), and he kindly gave me loads of information on the lake. The trip proved fruitless as far as putting fish on the bank, but I found it very interesting and certainly learned a lot. The challenge of these type of waters is exciting, although the approach needed for success borders on bloody hard work and requires the ability to endure fishing in uncomfortable circumstances. Maybe in the future I might give it another try.

I was back in the UK at the end of May and dying to get back on Korda Lake. Late May through June is really the best time to target tench as the fish will be feeding hard prior to spawning and the chance of a biggie is at its highest. This would also be the first time in years I had time off at this peak fishing time of the year, as the second leg of *The Legacy of the Beast* tour didn't start until July.

I'd been getting some reports from the lake. There had been some catches of tench, but no doubles so far. The weather was warm and settled but the fish had not been displaying any signs of spawning behaviour. I decided to have a real go at the pit, planning to spend three days and nights on the bank. Little did I know this session was to yield only one bite. But that bite was going to result in my long-awaited double-figure tench.

It was the morning of 28 May 2019, when I pulled in through the fishery gates. I had an area in mind, and on parking up I could see the swim I wanted was free. In fact, there were no other anglers on that particular bank at all. I drove around and parked up right behind the peg, which was in the middle of a causeway bank. I had fished the swim before, and knew there were plenty of features, the most obvious being two gravel bars that ran parallel to my bank, the first at 20 yards out and the second at around 50 yards. I planned to fish one rod on the top of the first bar and the other two on the back of the second, where the slope of the gravel levelled out on to firm silt. I'd heard a whisper that anglers had been doing well on worms, so I decided to go with a worm kebab rig in tandem with method feeders. My plan was to pile in lots of groundbait laced with worms, casters, hemp and a sprinkling of corn, and fish the feeders over the top. I also felt the groundbait should be dark, as the big old wary fish on this lake might shy away from light-coloured patches of bait on the bottom.

Fifty or so tangerine-sized balls of groundbait were moulded, then left to harden, while I set up a spod rod with a bait sling attached. These are just the job for getting the balls out to a distance without the frustration of broken elastic and the painful wraps on the knuckles you get from catapults. I put the rods out on the spots, then set about organising my camp, home for the next three days. Usually, I don't like committing myself to one area for long periods, but in this case it was a well-known fact that the tench liked to patrol up and down the bars in the pit. Hopefully one or two would settle on the bait and I would pick up a few bites. I also knew this approach had worked for other anglers in the past here so I thought it worth investing the time.

The rest of the day passed without incident, as did the follow-ing night. Indeed, nothing stirred for that first 48 hours. I stuck with my plan, though, topping up the spots at intervals. Surely the tench would be unable to resist the banquet? As usual, I got up early on the third morning, hoping to spot rolling or bubbling fish, but apart from a few shows further down towards the end of the pit, I didn't see too much to boost my confidence.

It was now mid-morning and the sun was getting higher in the clear blue sky when, out of the blue, one of the rods, which was fished out to the far bar, let out a few bleeps before trundling off, the spool spinning steadily. I lifted into the fish and wound down, trying to take as much stretch out of the line as I could to keep in touch with the fish at a distance. The rod hooped over with heavy resistance out in the depths. I pumped the fish closer, a solid slow-moving weight, and then, as the fish approached the deep clear margins, I felt the first of several heavy head shakes. Tench!

The fish was really digging now, making powerful surges to the overhanging bushes to my right, causing me to slam on extreme side strain, extending my arms out fully to gain an advantage. Finally, the fish gave up and allowed me to guide it over to my waiting net. I threw my rod down and looked into the net, grabbing the folds and lifting, desperate to confirm what I already knew. I had done it! There before me lay an enormous tench. Immaculate, deep chested, well proportioned. The stuff of dreams.

'Yeeeessss! Fucking get in!' I shouted, like some sort of caveman bellowing over a fresh kill.

I took a minute, looking at the fish now resting in the net. The search for a double had taken me, on and off, the best part of ten years. Probably a dozen venues having been tried, culminating in the mad trip to the Orient in France just the week before. But it's all about the journey sometimes, and I had enjoyed every minute of the ride. I'd caught loads of fish in the course of my obsession, and not only tench. I'd had huge bream, and carp to over 40lb.

'How big?' A voice stirred me from my reverie. I turned to see another angler walking into my swim.

'Oh, er, how did you . . . er . . . know I'd caught one?' I stuttered.

'We heard you shouting from the other end of the lake!' said the bailiff, Dougal, grinning and joining us now. 'Better weigh her then.'

It was 10lb 8oz. Like specimen fish of all species, it looked slightly surreal laid out on the mat, impossibly big somehow. Danny, the other angler, had a decent camera with him and we got some good shots of the giant. I managed a few with my iPhone also. Photo session over, I put the fish back in the landing net and placed it gently into the water. I stared at it for a few minutes. Then, lowering the net cord, I eased the fish forward and watched it waddle back down the marginal slope and disappear.

CHAPTER SIXTEEN

Fishing With Friends And Family

I've always been a bit of a loner when it comes to fishing. Whether it's because I'm quite spontaneous or I've had a few bad experiences with going fishing with friends, I don't know. By bad experiences, I'm not talking *Deliverance* here. More like someone talks you into a fishing trip, and then on the day moans, groans and wants to go home early. Either way, that type of thing put me off fishing with other people for a while.

I'm glad to say things have changed in the last 15 years or so and I've had some memorable trips away with friends. I even managed to get my brother Patrick out on the bank again after him not fishing for the best part of 40 years. I had booked a week in Mequinenza on the River Ebro in Spain and asked him in one of our quarterly phone chats if he fancied coming along. He had always taken an interest in my fishing exploits over the years, pumping me for details about my latest catches. (I didn't need much encouragement.) He was keen, especially after I told him tales of monster carp and catfish in Catalonia. I booked the flights, transport and accommodation (I have learned well from rock 'n' roll tour managers), and we set off for Luton Airport to catch our budget airline flight to Barcelona at the ungodly hour of 5am. The check-in staff were just this side of rude, as if the fact that you were on a cheap ticket didn't mean you warranted any respect. I was stung for my excess baggage, and then we were herded aboard the plane. Whips cracked and passengers' cries of anguish ignored in the undignified scramble for the best seats. That was the last time I flew with that particular budget airline.

Even in his slightly bleary-eyed condition, my brother's laconic wit was to the fore.

'I'll have my filet mignon well-done, please,' he told an unamused flight attendant as we took our seats. We giggled. That set the tone for the trip.

We caught plenty of fish, although Patrick struggled a little at first, as he was trying to pick up 40 years of slack. (See what I did there?) It made me think how fishing equipment has changed over the years. Stiff carp rods, bite alarms, hair rigs, boilies, spods – all innovations spinning off the carp boom of the last 30 years. The baitrunner-reel concept was totally alien to Patrick, and the first few runs resulted in him striking violently into thin air, having not engaged the baitrunner switch to take it out of free spool. The last reel he had used was the old centrepin he handed down to me! He soon got the hang of it all, though, and as the week passed he notched up some nice fish. He was also a throwback to when anglers had patience, sat by their rods and struck at an indication.

We certainly lived the dream that week. The accommodation, a two-storey house, was yards from the river. It didn't have much in the way of heating, so we'd take it in turns to run in and top up the fire (it turns out it gets bloody cold even in Spain in November). One evening, I reeled in just after dark, having started early that morning. I had got into some nice carp and decided a cold beer in front of the fire was better than rowing my bait out to the middle of the Ebro in the pitch dark. It was a cold evening and I suggested Patrick should come in too as I had bought a particularly fine Rioja the day before, and it had his name on it. I told you we were living the dream! He declined and said he was going to fish on for half an hour or so. I left him to it and went inside to start dinner. I had just finished peeling the spuds when Patrick came in and calmly announced that he had caught a carp, 'quite a decent one', he added. He disappeared back out into the inky blackness. I downed tools, put my thermals on and followed.

He had left the fish to sulk in the landing net, secured in the shallow margin of the river. I organised the mat, scales and sling to get ready for weighing. I heard Patrick wrestling with the net in the darkness, then come staggering towards me, arms outstretched. I could make out a large shape in the bottom of the fully extended net. He swung the net towards the mat and laid the fish down. Parting the mesh, I looked upon the biggest carp I'd ever set eyes on.

'I think you might have broken your personal best there.'

We weighed her: 44lb!

The significance of the number was not lost on us: 44lb was the weight of Dick Walker's famous record common carp, caught at Redmire Pool in the 1950s. It was an iconic fish and something we only dared dream about when we were both young anglers. Now, here was a fish of exactly the same proportions, in the flesh. And now, here we were, two brothers, all grown-up.

We had many subsequent trips and a few laughs along the way and still do, to this day. On another occasion we went to a venue in France that had two lakes, which we booked exclusively. Patrick decided to fish the smaller lake and I the bigger. He ended up hooking the same carp four times that week, landing it three times and losing it at the net once (though I think on that occasion he felt bad and was trying to lose it). We even had a name for it: 'Old Red'.

Another time we fished a lake near Le Mans. Once again we had the lake to ourselves. The fish didn't play ball that week, though, and with only a handful caught while fishing in the daytime only, we decided to fish in adjacent swims through the darkness on our last night. We would make a final effort to try and get one of the monsters we knew were in there. I don't usually like fishing nights, thinking that if a fish goes to the trouble of picking up your hookbait, the least you can do is be awake at the time. Also, whenever the rods are out and I zip up the bivvy door, I don't feel like I'm really fishing. More like camping or trapping.

But on this occasion, desperate measures were required. I think it was about 4am when I heard a right old commotion coming from the direction of Patrick's swim. My bite alarm let out a few bleeps but, even in my bleary state, I guessed what had happened. Patrick must have hooked one and it had run through my line. Sure enough, a few minutes later he appeared at my bivvy door.

'Er, I've caught one, Adrian. I think it's quite big . . .'

Judging by his appearance, he must have had a battle. His hat was hanging from his head, held in place only by the strap from his headtorch, which itself was pointing eccentrically straight up into the stars. His jacket was all askew. He really looked like he'd been in a scrap. I followed him back the few yards to his swim. My own torchlight revealed a tale of battle. Rods were strewn about, pointing at alarming angles, the rod pod was on its side, and a bucket of boilies looked like it had been booted into the lake.

'Bloody hell, what happened here?' I said.

But Patrick was already hauling the fish from the lake in the landing net. He plonked it on the mat and stepped back, breathless. The first thing that came to my mind when I saw that fish was that it resembled a halibut, as it seemed to be almost as deep as it was long. It was also very pale in colour. A typical French holiday fish. It was big, though, massive in fact: 52lb! *He's done it again*, I thought.

'That's the last time I'm inviting you fishing!' I joked.

Patrick never took up fishing full time again, despite his successes, but he's always happy to tag along with me on a trip. He'll always come out with a comment that cracks me up. Killing time on a long car ride in Spain, we were joking around thinking of funny film titles. Talking about a party of garishly dressed golfers we had seen that morning at the airport, he said, straight-faced, 'Ah yes. *The Land that Taste Forgot.*'

That had me grinning to myself for days.

Martin Connolly was another guy I reconnected with through fishing. 'Hippy Martin', as he is sometimes known, has been an avid carper and bass player for longer than he can remember. And when you've made the hippy pilgrimage to India as many times as Martin did in the 1960s and 1970s, you can be forgiven for forgetting the odd thing. I hadn't seen him for a number of years when he turned up at a Maiden gig. We talked shop for a while, as you do, and then the subject turned to fishing. Around that time, I was planning my first trip to Mequinenza, the place where I later went with Patrick. I asked Martin if he fancied joining me and he agreed.

We met up at Luton Airport for the flight to Barcelona. Martin is another bloke who comes out with some classic one-liners. We were standing in the check-in line, me in my green fishing togs and with too much fishing gear, as usual, and Martin dressed head to toe in black, tall and slim, with a mane of long black hair, though he's older than me. Not a lot older, he'll tell you. Martin's luggage consisted of a single, battered suitcase. It was ancient and covered in stickers, and looked like it would fall apart in a strong breeze. He saw me looking at it kind of sideways with a smirk on my face.

'Nuffink wrong with that, guv,' he said. 'That's the Delhi Express. Been everywhere with that, mate. Never let me down.'

The Delhi Express. Lovely.

That trip was memorable in that it was such a different fishing experience for both of us. We had rented a second-floor apartment in Mequinenza, a small town on the confluence of the rivers Ebro and Segre, about 90 minutes' drive west of Barcelona. The mornings were crisp and chilly, and from one balcony we could see the river, flanked on one side by huge, sand-coloured cliffs butting together with a bright blue sky. As we sat drinking our coffee we could see the odd carp crashing out.

'That'll do for me, guv,' said Martin, laughing. 'Let's get the gear ready.'

We struggled initially, though. The area we had been advised to fish certainly held plenty of big carp. The reason for this was that, before the big dam was built and the valley below flooded, the area had been an orchard. We were getting runs all right, but were having trouble landing them, in among the old tree stumps. It's funny, but when you fish somewhere for the first time and have little success, your mind starts playing tricks on you. I began to think that these carp were different. Silly really, as they were just carp, plain and simple. A fact about to be proved as a 4x4 came bumping down the track towards us.

It was Jürgen, one of the guys from the Bavarian Guiding Service. He enquired how we were doing, then asked if we minded if he fished with us for an hour. No probs, we said. Plenty of room (well, the Ebro is 200 miles long). Jürgen produced a carp rod from the rear of the truck. It was all rigged up, with an odd-looking bait hanging from his hair rig. Frolic, a dog-food pellet, was a much-used bait in the area, apparently. He lobbed the rig out into the Ebro and propped the rod up against a large white rock. He then disappeared into one of the allotments that bordered the river and came back a minute later with a length of plastic piping. Delving into his toolbox for a saw, he fashioned a throwing stick. *Bit resourceful, this chap*, we thought.

Jürgen then proceeded to catch two 30lb commons in the next couple of hours, while Martin and I sat biteless and inactive, apart from one or the other of us acting as net boys. He then bade us a cheery farewell, before driving off to pick up his kids from school, no doubt helping them with their homework, cooking dinner and repainting the house before turning in. As I said, a resourceful chap. Jürgen would become another fishing-related friend and still regularly turns up at Maiden shows with a busload of friends and family.

His haul had proved that these Ebro carp were only human after all, so to speak. Martin and I gradually got used to the fishing there and finished the week with a few good carp between us. We left for the long drive to Barcelona Airport chatting excitedly about our trip, and already planning the next one.

I went fishing with Thin Lizzy guitarist, Scott Gorham, once. Lizzy were one of my favourite bands growing up and the Robertson–Gorham guitar partnership was a massive influence. Brian Robertson was all street swagger and attitude, Gorham tasty and melodic, each complementing one another. Les Pauls in tandem, slung low, they were just so damn cool.

My only contact with Robbo was at a club in London back in the eighties when we literally bumped into each other. On that occasion, he actually squared-up to me, like I'd done it on purpose, though I suspect the reverse was true. Luckily, a mutual friend, Bernie Shaw, singer for rock veterans Uriah Heep, was present. Bernie, one of the music biz's truly nice guys, stepped in and introduced us, diffusing a potentially awkward situation. Either way it would have been a good story. 'I got chinned by Brian Robertson last night!'

I met Scott at a charity gig at the Thunderdrive in London in 1994. My wife Nathalie was organising the event along with tennis star Pat Cash and his wife Emily, and asked me to perform a couple of numbers on a bill that was to include Chrissie Hynde, the Cult and, bizarrely, Rolf Harris.

I didn't like jamming much in those days. Past experience had proved that these things usually descend into drunken self-indulgent 'free-for-alls'. Nathalie assured me that this would be more organised, so I agreed to play. The jam would also coincide with the Wimbledon tennis tournament. So, as well as known musicians performing, it would be a chance to see my old mate Pat Cash letting his hair down, as well as John McEnroe jamming with the likes of Chrissie Hynde. The evening was a roaring success, raising much-needed funds for the Vitas Gerulaitis Youth Foundation. The house band for the evening were a collection of rock veterans, including another old mate, ex-Urchin and FM guitarist, Andy Barnett.

A little later in the evening, I got up on stage with Nicko McBrain, bassist Gary Liedeman and me ol' mucker Dave Murray. It was packed and sweltering in the club as we ran through a short set that included Cream's 'Sunshine of Your Love', with me handling vocals as well as guitar. I was a bit edgy to start with. It's funny, but most musicians find it easier to perform in front of thousands of people in arenas than a few hundred punters in the more intimate setting of a club. The audience was also filled with music heavyweights such as Peter Gabriel, Rod Stewart, Jimmy Page and Jeff Beck. I'd also noticed Scott Gorham in the crowd, which didn't help ease my nerves! The set went well, though, and I was feeling good as I towelled off and had a beer backstage afterwards. Then Nathalie appeared and told me Scott had really enjoyed our set.

'We should get him up on stage. We could do "Rosalie"!' I enthusiastically commented.

With that, Nathalie turned on her heels to find Scott. She reappeared about 15 minutes later. 'Scott's going to jam with you,' she said. 'You're on in five!'

Jesus, I was going to jam with one of my idols. I downed the rest of my beer and made myself presentable. I pushed my way through the sweaty crowd to the stage just as Chrissie Hynde was ending her set. After the roadies had finished scurrying around tidying up tangled leads and rearranging mic stands, I climbed on to the small stage. I stood, tuning my guitar as various house-band members took up station on their instruments.

'Hey, man.'

I looked up. It was Scott.

'Hi! "Rosalie" in A then?' I said.

'Sure, man,' said Scott, Californian drawl to the fore.

We launched into the song, Scott ripping the solo and me singing the song I'd played a hundred times before in various bands. The crowd loved it, and afterwards Scott and I exchanged numbers and started a friendship that endures to this day.

Fast forwarding to the year 2000, Scott rang to say that a friend of his, Martin Bowley, managing director of Carlton TV at the time, had invited him on a corporate fly-fishing trip. Knowing I was a keen angler, he thought I would be interested.

Also, Scott had never fished before in his life so needed some moral support.

Two weeks later, I was driving down the M3 towards Hampshire to meet the guys. The plan was to stay the night at a nice country pub, before getting up early and heading to the beautiful River Test. Martin, Scott and I spent an enjoyable evening of pub grub and local beer. After talking Martin out of buying another round of drinks, we retired for the night.

The next morning after breakfast and plenty of coffee, we made the short drive to the river. Scott was a little apprehensive – to my amusement, I must admit. He needn't have worried though. He and Martin, who also had never fished, would be in the hands of an expert fly-fishing instructor and guide. On arrival, we were greeted by the sight of about 20 other anglers of varying degrees of skill, some no doubt more interested in the free drinks provided than the spectacular trout fishing. It certainly was an idyllic setting and underlined perfectly the difference, albeit an ever-decreasing one, between trout and coarse fishing, when the former was practised by the gentry and the latter by the great unwashed.

The mill house, a relic from another era, was the centrepiece. Beautifully preserved and renovated, it stood flanked by lush manicured lawns that sloped down to the river's edge. The river itself ran clear and pristine, the swaying weeds a vivid green in the current.

After a bit of a pep talk from the guides, everyone made their way to various locations along the river and its carrier streams. Scott and Martin went up to the mill pond for some casting lessons, and, anxious to avoid the crowd, I wandered off and found a nice stretch of water for myself. I spent a pleasant morning fishing down the beat, landing a nice brownie and also a blue trout of about 5lb, a first for me. The blue trout is a sort of mutant rainbow, and they fight incredibly hard. Happy with my morning session, I made my way back to the mill house for lunch.

Scott and Martin were already there and we went to sample the sumptuous three-course meal. They had enjoyed their morning and had landed some decent fish from the mill pool. We all headed off again after lunch, with Martin telling me that legendary broadcaster David Frost was going to be fishing later that afternoon. 'Be back around five,' he said. 'I'll introduce you.'

Of course, it was around 8pm when I eventually made it back to the lodge. I'd become so engrossed in the fishing I'd forgotten all about meeting the TV icon. Martin and Scott were standing by the cars, getting ready to leave, when I traipsed up.

'You really are keen, aren't you?' chorused the guys, laughing.

I asked Scott if he was now going to become an angler, already kind of knowing the answer . . .

'I think I'll stick to golf.'

I thanked them for the invite and we said our goodbyes. They headed back to London. And me? I headed back to Lymington to have a crack at the big roach in Sway Lakes.

Having grown up with a father who was a keen angler, I couldn't wait to get my son Dylan out on the bank. Although he would happily come along with me, he never really took to fishing like I did when I was a boy. Maybe it was a generational thing. Kids have so many other distractions now, computers mainly.

We have had quite a few trips away together, though, and once out he enjoys a bit of angling. He was with me when I landed my first 20lb carp at a lake in Belgium, in 1999. Fishing was always a good way to spend some quality time together.

In late summer of 2006, we went for a week's carping in France. I had rented a small lake with fish up to mid-30-pounders and a comfortable house nearby to sleep in. We had a great week with plenty of action. On the second to last evening we wound in, leaving the tackle at the lake, and made the short drive back to the house. We planned to have a quick freshen-up before heading to dinner. It was dark when we pulled up outside the accommodation in the little village and hurried inside, hungry and anxious to get to the restaurant before it closed. Ten minutes later, when we went back outside and the car had gone.

An empty space stood where I'd left it on the cambered grass verge opposite the house.

'Someone's bloody nicked it! Can you believe it? In the middle of nowhere!' I stood hands on hips looking this way and that.

'Dad, I think I see it,' Dylan said, while making his way forward down the deserted and now pitch-black road, using the torch on his phone.

I followed Dylan and there was the car. Its front bumper imbedded slightly into the side of a parked Transit van.

'How the hell . . . ? What?'

I was puzzled. Then it clicked. I had rented a car with a manual transmission, which I wasn't used to driving, and I'd forgotten to put the handbrake on and left it in neutral. I imagined the scenario: Dyl and I in the house, and the car minus the driver rolling ghostly and hearse-like down the narrow lane. Luckily, out of all the cars it could have crashed into, the van it hit belonged to the lake owner, Pascal. The damage was minimal and when I told him the next day he just laughed and told me not to worry. He did say that maybe I should let my son drive from now on.

Dylan did get very interested in another passion of mine: music. With guitars, drums and bass lying around the house when he was growing up, he got pretty competent on all of them. Production engineering and mixing became his primary focus, and when he was around 20 I thought it was time he tasted a bit of road life. So in 2009 he joined the Maiden crew for the *Somewhere Back in Time* tour. Looking back, maybe he was thrown in at the deep end. The crew work hard. They have to be at the venue first thing in the morning, then pack all the gear away before climbing back on the bus in the early hours of the morning to journey to another show. That is the routine for three straight months. Still, I think Dylan learned something, even if it was that he didn't want to be a roadie.

I pretty much left him to it on the road, though I know everyone on the crew was keeping an eye on him. We did meet up for dinner on nights off, and even managed to get out fishing in Ecuador. Quito, the capital city, is situated in the foothills of the Andes Mountains. The tour up to that point had been fun but hectic, and I was desperate for some peace and quiet. After doing some research on the net, I was surprised to learn that there was trout fishing available not far from Quito itself. I had our tour manager, Ian Day, call the promoter, who fixed us up with a day's fishing at Campuchoca Lodge, about an hour's drive from the capital.

It was a warm, pleasant morning when Dylan and I climbed aboard the van that was to take us up to the lodge. Quito is almost two miles above sea level, but our destination would take us even further up into the foothills. We had packed some warm clothes as we'd been told it would feel considerably colder up there. On arrival at Campuchoca Lodge, we were greeted by owner Eduardo Campuzano, a retired businessman, and our guide for the day, Andreas. They were right about the cold. Although the sun shone brightly, the blustery wind that blew down the mountain valley was ice cold. We donned fleeces and windbreakers and made our way to the first lake with Andreas after Eduardo had headed off, saying he'd meet us later for lunch. We were handed a couple of 5-weight outfits loaded with 'sinktip' line and a large streamer fly attached to some heavy mono. The lake was probably around two acres and had been created by redirecting the water and damming one of the steep ravines nearby. It was one of several lakes crafted by Eduardo and he had stocked them with fry from some of the higher elevation natural lakes. We punched our streamers out into the peat-coloured water, battling the increasingly violent wind. We were into trout almost immediately. Rainbows, mostly in the 1 to 1½lb bracket, smashed our flies with wild abandon.

After fishing through the morning we made our way up to the main lodge to join Eduardo for lunch. Sitting on the veranda overlooking the mountains, he told us how he had left the city and a life as a successful businessman to create his Ecuadorian fishing paradise. There were, he said, some natural lakes about a 20-minute hike from the lodge that contained larger trout. Did we want to try one of them this afternoon? Hunger satisfied, we loaded up with our tackle and followed Eduardo up a rough trail towards the lake. As we climbed even higher, Dylan and I had to stop occasionally as we traversed a particularly steep section. If you are not used to it, exertion at high altitude can be hard work, oxygen being less plentiful. Meanwhile, Eduardo who must have been getting on for 70, forged ahead like a frisky young mountain goat. The effort was worth it, though. The lake was beautiful. Blue water gave way to green hills rolling down to the shoreline, with the Andes Mountains in the background.

It is home to pumas, bears and the mighty condor, one of the largest birds in the world.

The plan was to go afloat trolling streamers and nymphs, with Eduardo manning the oars. Luckily, the wind had died down a little and we managed to land some of the most beautifully marked and hard-fighting rainbow trout I had ever encountered. As promised, these fish were bigger, with the best maybe going on 3½lb. With their vivid crimson slash, blue-green sheen and jet-black spots, these fish certainly gave us an afternoon to remember.

As the light was fading, we made our way down the mountain. Back at the lodge, I popped upstairs to use the loo. When I looked in the mirror, I was shocked to discover that the right side of my face was bright red, particularly from the cheek back to the ear. We were so cold when fishing that the last thing I thought about was getting sunburned, but now I had a bad case of it. In fact, my cheek area stayed red and inflamed for the next two years, resulting in my needing treatment for skin damage.

Over dinner that night, back at the hotel in Quito, Dylan and I reflected on our day out. It was a unique experience, and once again my travels had allowed me to sample fishing in another wild and wonderful location. I'll bring the sunblock next time though.

CHAPTER SEVENTEEN

High Jinks On The Lower Trent

The River Trent is one of England's longest rivers. Rising in Staffordshire, it flows, wide and powerful, through Notting-hamshire and Derbyshire, eventually joining the River Ouse, Humber and then on to the North Sea. In the late nineteenth century, it still had a thriving salmon fishery, until developments following the Industrial Revolution led to heavy pollution along much of its length. By the mid-1970s, the Trent, like a lot of British rivers, had begun to recover, due in part to the economic recession. The closures and cutbacks in heavy industry and tighter pollution laws helped the waterway to recover.

And recover it has, as it is probably the best river for specimen fish in the UK. At this moment, species such as chub, barbel, pike, zander and roach all grow to massive proportions in the now rich, clean water, and every week the angling press is full of large Trent fish.

This rise in the Trent's profile hadn't gone unnoticed by me and I spent a lot of my downtime on the road scanning the internet for more information on the river. *The Book of Souls* world tour, which started on 24 February 2016, was due to finish on 22 July 2017. I have to say, at times, it was one of the hardest tours I've ever done.

The specially kitted-out Ed Force One Boeing 747 was massive, and it did make life easier in some ways. The band and management had the front section and also the upstairs, if anyone wanted to sleep. The crew had the whole mid-to-back section and there was also a space midway down the plane where you could almost have had a game of five-a-side football. Some of the lads might have even tried this after sampling too much of the free bar . . .

So, all sounds great, right? It did have some downsides. Running a big plane like that isn't cheap! Every hour you are on the ground costs money, so you've just got to keep rolling; days off became travel days, and not just hops. On completing the whole South, Central and North American tour with two shows in Los Angeles, we flew straight to Tokyo the morning after. Japan went well, albeit in a blur. Then we flew to China for shows in Beijing and Shanghai.

By the time we reached Shanghai, I didn't know which way was up. I tried to get myself going by taking a walk with the missus in Shanghai. We got a taxi to the local market, with Nathalie's brother Marc and his wife Quottnim, as they wanted to sample some local food and stroll the bustling streets. After only about five minutes, I stepped off the pavement without looking and almost walked straight under a bus. It was only Nathalie pulling me back that avoided a very nasty incident. I was so tired and jetlagged, I couldn't function. So I left the guys and took a taxi back to the hotel. I shut the curtains and jumped into bed. Flying almost every day puts a lot of strain on your body and any aches and pains you are carrying get magnified tenfold. My knees and back ached constantly.

I don't think any of us were looking forward to playing in China. I had heard stories of horrible stomach bugs among other things, but the shows went well. The Beijing audience was quite reserved. You could tell they were enjoying the music and the show, but they were unsure how to react. Each song was given a quiet round of applause but you could see from the big smiles from the audience that they were into it. Before the show there were local police backstage. Our manager Rod came into the dressing room as we were getting changed. He looked serious – not unusual for our Rod – but there was something going on.

He told us the police had instructed him that there was to be no smoking or drinking on stage. OK. We don't anyway, apart from Dave and I having an occasional tipple before the encores. Also, he said that we weren't to throw guitar picks or wristbands into the audience or 'incite' them in any way.

'Are we allowed to have any fun?' I joked.

Now, we always joke that Yorkshireman Rod is the rock 'n' roll equivalent of Sir Alex Ferguson, and he has been known to dish out the 'hairdryer' treatment if you raise his ire.

'Give me a fooking break, H!' he bellowed in my direction. 'It's China, what do you expect?'

Oops. I wasn't the only one who was a bit tired. All right then . . .

Shanghai was very different, with more Westerners in the audience. We were met with a more typical rock-type reaction.

The next day we loaded up the plane and headed for New Zealand. I had been looking forward to getting to Christchurch. We had a day off and, having done some research, I had found out that our hotel had a stream running through the park opposite. The only fly in the ointment was the small matter of a 13-hour flight from Shanghai to Christchurch. We arrived in New Zealand even more tired and jetlagged. The hotel we were staying at was a bit 'Fawlty Towers' but the location was good. New Zealand is like England 50 years ago. It made a nice change from the concrete jungles of Japan and China.

Now, before you tell me off about getting all snobby about hotels, here are a few facts about life on the road.

1. Twenty-four-hour room service is a must. No, this is not rock-star mollycoddling. When you're knackered and maybe just have got off a plane or sweated your nuts off on stage for two hours, the last thing you want to do is traipse around some city you don't know, looking for a bite to eat.

2. Cleanliness is next to godliness. I expect the place I'm staying in to be as clean as my house. I can't handle dirty cutlery, cups, etc., or air-conditioning vents all clogged up with mould, or pubic hairs (not yours) in the bed. Once, in England, I was washing my hands in the toilets of a hotel lobby. Somebody was in the stall, and from the sound of it was having some, er . . . intestinal problems. Said man then emerged from the cubicle. He was in full chef's uniform, big white hat, the lot. He looked at me, exhaled hard, then said, 'Blimey, that's better!' Then he turned on his heels and went straight out of the door, not going near the washbasin.

3. Thou shalt not start drilling holes in the room next door at eight in the morning. You'd be surprised how often this happens, even in good hotels. They are quite happy to take your money, but then forget to tell you they're remodelling the hotel during your stay. This happened to me in a five-star hotel in Oslo when I was awoken by hammering and drilling early one morning. On checking out, I complained about it. As I turned to leave, the frumpy old girl on reception half-whispered, half-said, 'Maybe you should get up earlier.' Unbelievable! I had to be restrained . . . I could go on.

I did manage to get out fishing for a few hours in Christchurch. The stream running through the park was like a miniature

Hampshire Avon. I saw some nice brown trout but couldn't get one to eat my fly. I suspected that these fish had probably seen every trick in the book. Streetwise, if you like. Still, it was a nice break out in the fresh air. That was the only bit of fishing I was able to do on that leg of the tour. No complaints as we were supposed to be working.

The tour rolled on through Australia and then on to South Africa, a first for me. Eventually, it was straight back on the plane and onwards towards Europe to start the next leg of the tour. I was looking forward to Dortmund, Germany, as I had a fishing mate in Oberhausen. I'd met Lutz when he'd been a guide on a salmon-fishing trip I did in Norway. We also had a mutual love of blues music and, in between blanking on the salmon river, we'd jam blues tunes on a couple of old acoustics he had lying around.

I'd arranged to hook up with Lutz on the day before the show and got a car to take me the 30 minutes or so from Dortmund to Oberhausen. Lutz was now guiding on the River Ahr, a trout stream that winds its way through beautiful country, rolling green fields and vineyards.

We met up around lunchtime by an old cobbled bridge in the village. Lutz's lovely wife, Sarah, came along to say hello and we all made a plan to meet for dinner later. Lutz then motioned for me to come and have a look over the bridge. There below, finning in the current just behind a clump of weeds, was a large rainbow trout.

'Big Mamma!' said Lutz, his permanent grin even wider. 'We come back later.'

We headed off downstream and spent the rest of the afternoon catching trout and catching up.

'Wonder how Mamma's doing?' I offered.

Lutz grinned. 'Want to have a try?'

'Might as well.'

We made our way back to the bridge.

I'd like to say that I crept into position, executed a perfect cast, and that the big trout rose and sucked in my dry fly . . . but it didn't. Despite throwing every fly I had, and catching every other trout in the pool, she would not oblige.

Lutz was leaning over the bridge, his grin now at its maximum wideness.

'Schlau!' he said.

Schlau — smart — indeed.

'She's cunning,' said Lutz.

Oh yeah.

I finally gave up on that trout. The hunger pains were kicking in. We made our way into the village where we were to meet up at the local winery for dinner with Lutz's wife and some of their friends. We sampled the delicious local wines (not too much as I had a show the next day) and ate a traditional meal of sausage, potato and sauerkraut. A nice end to a nice day. As for Big Mamma, she's become a standing joke between us and I always ask how she is when I email Lutz, as I would ask after a family member.

The touring schedule became a lot easier with short hops between gigs in Europe. The jetlagged haze of the last few months lifted and days off were spent sightseeing instead of lying in bed, comatose with the curtains drawn.

On the music front, we were all really enjoying playing the set. It had a lot of variations in feel and tempo and gave me personally a bit more room to let my playing breathe. I thought 'If Eternity Should Fail' was a great opener. It was dramatic and powerful without being frantic, and it gave everyone a chance to settle into the show. I thought it was very ballsy of Bruce to open the show like that on his own, though it did come about by accident. During rehearsals for the tour, Bruce started singing along with the intro tape, just to warm his voice up, I think. It sounded good so he decided to do it during the show. I must admit I got a little emotional when I watched him do it at that first gig. As I stood there with my guitar, side-stage, waiting to run on, I started to well up. Watching him out there on his own made me think of the battle he had fought the previous year when he discovered he had throat cancer. Now, here he was, back again. Of course, after a few weeks we were back to normal with myself, Dave and our techs, Sean and Colin, messing about like schoolboys behind the curtain during the intro.

The tour rolled on through Europe, and we were joined by my son's band Wild Lies for the two Download shows in Paris and the UK. It was great having Dylan out for a few days and they got the full rock-star treatment, coming on the big plane with us to Donington, where they played a storming set in the Red Bull Tent.

The last show was at the Wacken Festival in Germany. We were all a bit fried by this point so I wasn't happy to hear the whole show was going to be streamed live all over the world. No pressure then! We could have done without it but you just have to get on and do the show. Trouble is, you're aware of the fact you're being televised so it can be distracting. You end up thinking about what you're doing too much, instead of just going for it. Also, rock bands, especially heavy rock, don't come across on TV that well. Television sterilises and processes heavy rock for me, and the small speakers in a laptop or TV don't help. On the other hand, I'm proud of the live DVDs Maiden have done, at least when the sound is mixed properly and it does the band justice. How many times have you heard a live broadcast where one of the guitars is missing or all you can hear is vocals?

We flew straight back to the UK after the show for some much-needed rest and relaxation. The next leg of the tour didn't start until April 2017, so I was looking forward to catching up with friends and family, and of course dusting off the fishing rods. It was then that I starting fishing for tench on Korda Lake, which took up much of the summer and autumn.

By the time mid-October came around I was starting to think about the rivers, the Trent in particular. My fishing mate Spug had never caught a barbel, so we made a plan to do a couple of days on the river at the South Muskham Fishery, Nottinghamshire.

Spug, aka Mike Redfern – the name had piqued my curiosity. I'd read some of his articles in the carp magazines and seen him holding some vast carp up for the camera. He was also a Maiden fan and he'd sent me one of his books, along with an invitation to join him on a session at the famous Fox Mere. I was hesitant at first. After all, I'd never met the chap and if we didn't get along the prospect of 48 hours fishing together . . . well, it might be a bit awkward to say the least. We swapped emails and talked on the phone. We talked freely, the way fishermen often do. He seemed like a good bloke, funny and obviously mad on his carp fishing, and after another email from him featuring some big old mirrors from the Mere, I decided to take him up on his kind offer. The Fox Mere trip went well, and over the subsequent years we have had enjoyable trips out after zander, tench and even bream.

Our excursion to the Trent at Muskham was not that productive in terms of fish. He did catch his first barbel, and was understandably chuffed. (Well, he got the best peg that time!)

It was a learning experience. The Trent is a powerful river and my 1¾lb barbel rods were a bit on the light side. I couldn't get settled as the leads, either 3oz or 4oz, would get dragged out of place after 20 minutes or so. I'd also just taken long bank sticks to mount my buzzers on, and the rods had to be put at such a steep angle to keep the line off the water, that they weren't really stable enough. Spug was using his 'shark' gear, heavy 3½lb carp rods and 5oz leads. This at least meant he could fish efficiently and hold his hookbait in the hotspot next to the sunken barge on his far bank.

A solitary chub hung itself on one of my rods. I didn't even see the bite. It was just 'on' when I reeled in. We had a laugh, and were comfortably bivvied up on the bank with our cars parked conveniently behind us. We met a few of the local anglers and pumped them for knowledge, of course. One chap we met was a mine of information. He had parked on the track behind us and stopped for a chat. With him being a local, we listened closely as he regaled us with stories of his barbel exploits and gave us snippets of all-important information.

Then the subject changed from fishing to footie. OK, that's fine. Then he started telling us his life story. Well, that's okay, too, but after about half an hour of this, I felt the will to live draining from my body. Then he started talking about his new, much younger wife and how he felt sexually rejuvenated. Ah . . . I looked at Spug and rolled my eyes as this chap exclaimed, 'And the foreplay! My favourite!' Now, I'm not a prude but when a complete stranger starts talking to me about foreplay . . . I made my excuses and retired to my bivvy. As I lay down on my bedchair, I heard him say, 'And 'er skin's as soft as silk!' in his broad Notts accent. I zipped up the door and pulled the sleeping bag over my head.

Our next sortie to the Trent was to be at Collingham. We had booked 48 hours on the famous weir pool and this time there would be four of us. We were joined by Spug's mate and current golden orfe record holder, Lawrence King, and former Great Britain decathlete, Dean Macey. As the trip grew near, excitement mounted, such was the reputation of the fishing on

Collingham. The weir pool itself produces more double-figure barbel than just about anywhere else in the UK. The downside, of course, is that the pool is fished heavily and swims are booked up to a year in advance. To say we were looking forward to it would be an understatement. We even set up our own little Facebook group for the event. In the weeks leading up to the trip we swapped fish pics, discussed the merits of fishing gear and generally wound ourselves up to fever pitch. I'm usually pretty spontaneous about my fishing, preferring short sessions, grabbing a few rods and bait when the chores are done and the weather's right. Actually, come to think of it, I'll go fishing instead of doing any of my chores and when the weather's crap. But I have to admit there's something special about looking forward to a planned fishing trip.

Nottingham's a three-hour drive for me, so I travelled up the night before, planning to overnight in a guesthouse. Dean and Spug were bivvied up and fishing the stretch below the weir already, so I popped round to see them on my way to the guesthouse. I drove to the swims down a bumpy dirt road in the pitch black, eventually managing to find Spug. He'd been fishing for a few hours but so far no luck. He wound in his rods and suggested we go down and see Dean. Dean was camped up about a hundred yards downstream. Approaching his bivvy, Spug called out and a tall figure emerged. He bounded over to greet us, thrusting out a large hand. He exuded health and energy and this impression was reinforced by the flame-coloured bobble hat atop his head. After a brief chat we left him to it. Spug and I wandered off to make a cup of tea. Halfway through the brew, Spug's phone rang.

'Macey's 'ad one,' he said, thumb raised.

We went back to Dean's peg, trying not to spill our tea as we hurried along the bank in the dark. We arrived in his swim.

'How big?' we enquired.

'Dunno,' said Deano in broad Canvey. 'Ain't got me 'eadtorch!'

Fully torched-up, I peered into the landing net. There followed a barrage of expletives, as in the bottom of the net was a very big chub. On the scales it went: 6lb 14oz. A veritable clonker and a great start to the trip.

I bade them goodnight and headed for my hotel. Perhaps the word hotel was misleading, as it was more of a bed & breakfast. It was run by a retired couple who'd rented out their college-bound kids' rooms. The lady seemed nice enough. She showed me to my room and flicked the light switch. A single fluorescent tube on the ceiling spluttered into life.

'OK?' she said.

'It will be when we get the heating on!' I quipped. The room was freezing.

'Oh. It is on,' she said, pointing to a tiny radiator on the wall. 'Breakfast's seven till nine,' she said cheerily and bustled out of the room.

B&Bs . . . gotta love 'em.

Just before turning in, I got a text from Spug. He'd caught his first double-figure barbel. I texted back my congratulations and got my head down.

I rose early the next day and, after foregoing breakfast (I can't face piles of greasy bacon and eggs first thing in the morning), I drove the short distance to meet the chaps near the weir pool. Spug introduced me to Lawrence, and everyone was in high spirits as we unloaded piles of tackle onto straining barrows. One by one, everyone made their way up the half a mile or so of rough track to the pool. Everyone except me. I had brought four pints of maggots to try. I thought I'd be clever and try the grubs, as mostly everyone uses pellets and boilies at Collingham. Unfortunately, I hadn't secured the lid properly and some of the maggots had escaped in the back of my car. I watched in horror as they burrowed enthusiastically into every nook and cranny. They almost looked happy, well, as happy as maggots could get. I spent the next half an hour trying to get all of the little buggers out of the car but it was a losing battle. In a few weeks, I'd have a plague of flies in my 4x4, which is like a travelling shed at the best of times. No wonder my missus refuses to ride in it.

Eventually I was packed and ready. I wasn't messing around this time. I'd brought two Martin Bowler 2lb test-curve barbel rods and a Korum River rod pod. I huffed and puffed my way up to the pool. Dean was already there and even had his bivvy up, perhaps having already set a new world-record time for the Collingham half-mile dash. The guys had already decided on their swims.

This is always a bit tricky when you're fishing with mates. When I have a look at a section of water, there's always a swim that I really fancy. Chances are that your mate will want it, too. I suppose you should be a gentleman and offer first choice to your friend. Or, you could, while standing in said swim with said friend, remark casually that it's the worst swim on the river, full of snags, someone got murdered there once, etc., but hey, if you want it, no problem . . .

But as I wasn't going to be fishing nights, they had put me in the best peg, the first one nearest the weir sill, with Lawrence on the next swim downstream, then Spug, and Dean a bit further down. The bailiff came around for a chat and advised me to chuck at least one rod as close as I could to the sill. He also said the barbel moved out of the weir during the night and fed downstream. This would give Spug and Dean a crack at them as well. The morning was sunny and cold, but clouds and rain were forecast for the afternoon and the next day, before a cold snap moved in on the day of our departure. Perfect! I got myself organised and prepared to cast my first rod. I'd been thinking about my set-up and had come up with an idea I thought would work well. Along with the two Bowler rods, I had Daiwa reels loaded with 12lb line. To this I attached my end tackle which I'd christened the Flying Turd Rig. This was basically a helicopter style rig with a detachable lead. It enabled me to thread a long PVA stocking of freebie baits up the leadcore and then reattach the lead to hold it in place. The rubber beads buffering the hooklength swivel were then pulled down tight to the top of the stocking for further stability and finally the hook itself was nicked into the bag.

Having given it some thought, I guessed this rig would give me a good tangle-free presentation. Also, when the PVA stocking was filled with small halibut pellets, it resembled a large turd and thus excellent banter fodder.

I donned my waders and made my way out into the pool as far as I dared. I lined up the cast and the powerful rod sent the rig flying to the edge of the white water towards the sill, landing within a few yards with a reassuring crack onto the gravel.

'That's a bite,' I said to anyone who was listening.

I did the same with the other rod, only this time a large halibut pellet was the hookbait rather than the fishmeal boilie that was on the first rod. With both rods placed on the pod, it was time to sit back and put the kettle on. Spug and Lawrence busied themselves getting their rods out. Dean didn't seem in a great hurry and wandered along the bank, large grin and electric-orange bobble-hat prominent. The bailiff reckoned his swim wouldn't be productive during the day so Dean cannily just fed his peg with the intention of casting out at dusk. A very good decision as it turned out.

I'd just got myself comfortable in my chair with a brew when one of my buzzers omitted a few bleeps, then tore off. I grabbed the rod and pulled into the fish, feeling a satisfying thump as I did so. Everyone gathered round, eager for a glimpse of our first Collingham barbel. After a typically spirited scrap, the fish was in the net. A decent one too. On the scales it weighed

9lb 11oz. Next in was Lawrence with a double. Lawrence and I caught fish at intervals all day, including a real old warrior for me at 11lb 7oz. Spug was yet to get off the mark but wasn't too worried as he was still basking in the glow of his first double from the previous night. Dean, well, he just kept trickling in the bait over to the far side of the river – the spot he was going to start fishing as the light faded. As day slipped into night, so Lawrence's and my pegs died. Spug, though, had his first run and landed a barbel just into double figures. Happy with that, he re-cast his rod, and set about preparing a meal for dinner.

Then we heard Dean call up from downstream. He was into a fish as well. Cooking was put on hold as we all trooped down to his swim to have a look. Dean was standing up to his waist in the river and playing what was obviously a very good fish. What followed was one of the most amazing 40 minutes I've ever seen when fishing. Dean waded further out into the river to land the fish and sloshed back to the bank with his prize. In the net it was a huge barbel, 14lb 4oz to be precise. With the photos done, the fish was released and bolted powerfully back to the depths. After much back-slapping and congratulations, Dean re-baited and re-cast his rod back out into the far bank spot he had been feeding. He'd just placed the rod back on the pod when his other rod signalled a bite. Once again, he waded out to do battle with a big fish. A short while later, another Collingham barbel was in the net.

Then the unthinkable happened. His remaining rod hooped over and he was in again. Back out he went, while Lawrence scarpered up the bank for another landing net. This time I waded out alongside Dean to net the barbel for him as even he (twice Commonwealth Games gold medallist) was getting a bit knackered by then. We staggered back to the bank to weigh the second barbel: 14lb 7oz. Then we hoisted up the third fish in the weighsling. There was momentary silence as we waited for the needle on the scale to settle: 14lb 4oz. In a hectic 40 minutes, Mr Macey had landed three 14lb barbel. An amazing feat of angling, and the three of us there to witness it. Once he had calmed down a bit, Dean re-cast his rods but there was to be no more action for him that night.

Where were we? Oh yes, Spug had been cooking dinner . . . After all the excitement, he'd gone back to his peg to resume cooking duties while the rest of us pulled up our chairs around the fire and opened various bottles of wine and beer.

The four of us sat, with Spug, Master of Ceremonies, wielding the spatula, turning over sizzling steaks and pork chops while seated in his bivvy doorway. An ideal scene it was. Four anglers, out doing what they loved doing best, their contented expressions lit by the glowing fire, their head torches cutting swathes through the night. Also cutting swathes through the air was the banter between Lawrence and Spug. Let's say it was 'lively'. Nothing wrong with a bit of banter among friends. Just make sure they are good friends.

When I was 16, I worked in a lumber yard. It was my first proper job. The men who worked there were rough working-class guys and the banter was savage. I wouldn't dare open my mouth, but at the same time I kind of admired the swagger and bravado of these men. Most of the banter was good-natured but some of the guys could be nasty to the young kids. On one occasion I attempted to join in the proceedings.

The room where I worked housed all the big, wood-moulding machines. The noise of the cutting blades grinding against the wood as it was fed in was deafening, and you had to shout to be heard. Sometimes there would be an enormous cracking sound as one of the blades hit a knot in the wood and everyone would dive for cover. This was because we were terrified one of the blades would break and go flying across the shop. So much for Health & Safety.

There was a machinist called Ginger, a redheaded guy who was always joking around and seemed nice enough. A group of guys had gathered near him as he was feeding heavy six-foot cone planks of wood into the machine. My mate Norman, a couple of years older than me, was stacking the finished pieces on to a four-wheeled dolly. The banter was in full flow at Ginger's end. Here was my chance to be one of the 'guys'.

'Nearly missed that one, Ginge!' I shouted.

Ginger stopped what he was doing, looked at me, stone-faced, looked at the men at his end, and then back at me. He switched off the machine, dusted himself off and walked over. He leaned down and put his face to mine.

'Don't ever take the piss out of me,' he said, and he shoved me hard, his hands banging into my chest. I stumbled backwards and fell. Ginger stood over me, glaring, before walking slowly back to his machine. The men watching me drifted off. I was burning with rage and embarrassment. Norman helped me to my feet and I walked off, my mind racing.

Banter . . . just don't take on a big dog if you're still a pup, even though that particular big dog was just a bully. This incident stayed with me and for a good few years after that I was always wary when the banter started flying. I think the point is that my parents were right, of course, when they said I left school too early. On the other hand, incidents like that can be motivating in an 'I'll show him!' kind of way. On the other, other hand, my life would have been quite different had Ginger decided to feed me headfirst into the wood-moulding machine . . .

Meanwhile back at the camp, the night was still and quiet, save for the rush of the water tumbling over the weir. Then a howling bite alarm split the night and we swung our heads as one to see one of Spug's rods bouncing on the rest. What happened next is a bit of a blur. After the 'event' we all had a good laugh piecing together all the bits we remembered. It went something like this.

On hearing the bite alarm, Spug jumped from his chair and bolted towards the river with eyes only for his rod, which was bucking away, reel clutch sizzling. Unfortunately, he'd forgotten the small matter of a flaming barbecue in his path, resulting in him colliding with it at speed, sending chops, chicken wings and burning embers flying in all directions. The rest of us dived for cover, mouths agape in disbelief, while poor Spug lay spread-eagled on the ground. His head was raised up from the dirt, eyes still glued on the rod and unfinished business. His legs scrambled for purchase on the sandy terrain, and he righted himself and sprinted the remaining ten yards or so to his rod. He then commenced playing the fish, which incredibly was still attached.

Spug is a very good angler – he's caught more big carp than most, including the famous 'Two-tone' from Conningbrook at 56lb 8oz – but he doesn't take himself too seriously, which was just as well at this particular moment, because seeing the barbecue go flying and Spug scrambling away was hilarious. I think Dean was on his back laughing. Lawrence smelled blood and was unleashing a stinging volley of derision. Me, I thought I'd better go and help Spug land the fish. A medium-sized barbel. Spug guided the barbel over my waiting net, a stoic expression on his face, along with an occasional wince as someone fired a comment: 'Yer bum's on fire, Spug!'

Even Spug was laughing once we'd had a tidy-up and got the food back on.

I retired to my bed around 11pm. I didn't put my rods out, intending instead to get some sleep. I planned to get up early and start fishing again. I don't sleep too well on a bed-chair at the best of times but this night was made worse by being woken up every half an hour or so by a painful hip condition caused by bursitis. Despite having lugged my 'wide boy' bed-chair all the way to the weir from the car park, I was experiencing a deep, throbbing ache in my left hip. I was a bit shattered the next morning, to say the least.

The morning was bright and cold. The weather forecast had been spot on. The other guys were already up and I could hear muted conversation and the occasional guffaw, probably discussing last night's events. I got up and wandered down, zombie-like, to Spug's peg and the smell of frying bacon. Dean and Lawrence, like amateur detectives at a murder scene, were pointing to the marks on the sandy ground outside Spug's bivvy.

'That's where you fell over, mate,' said D.C. Macey, 'and two little 'oles are where you dug your feet in.' Good clean fun.

Nobody had enjoyed any action during the night. After breakfast, I went back to my swim and re-cast the rods. With the change in weather, the fishing slowed down, though I did manage a couple of small barbel in the afternoon. I decided to pack up that evening. I didn't fancy another night on the bank with my hip giving me problems. I had booked a hotel, planning to go and investigate another stretch further upstream the following morning. The other guys were going to fish the night, but had to be off the fishery at 7am because another party of anglers had booked the weir for the next two days. It had been a great trip, with plenty of action and laughs. I bade the guys farewell, Lawrence helping me back to the car park with my overloaded barrow.

CHAPTER EIGHTEEN

Bonefish
And
The Reverend

It's the beginning of 2016 and I am looking out of a second-floor balcony window on a private island in the Turks and Caicos. Directly in front is the home flat, a shallow sand-bottomed expanse, covered at this point – high tide – by two feet of water. Sometimes, early morning usually, you'll see a large bonefish cruising. But now the shadow of a four-foot sand shark moves purposefully across the bottom. No self-preserving bonefish will be there now.

I force my attention from the water back to my guitar and the business at hand. Maiden's *The Book of Souls* tour kicks off in a couple of weeks and, after not playing 'in anger' for almost six months, I'm trying to play for at least two hours a day in preparation. My practice routine has varied over the years from almost nothing to head down non-stop playing for three hours. Once, when trying to get 'on top of it' before a tour, I played a whole Maiden set through on an acoustic guitar with heavy strings, solos and all, for two weeks prior to rehearsals. It was effective too, though not a great deal of fun. I have over the years learned the benefits of practising and preparation, and I can't believe it took me so long to establish a routine. I think my approach to the guitar was heavily influenced by the fact that I was a vocalist/guitarist for the first five or so of my formative years.

High tide, and I'm not fishing yet. When the tide starts to run out, I'll make my way down to the dock, packing some sunscreen, water and fishing gear. A five-minute run in the skiff will take me to the edge of a large flat, just where it meets the boating channel. When the tide starts to run off, the bonefish will head off of the flat for the channel. They will have been feeding up in the mangroves, aggressively chasing crabs, shrimp and small fish. Here, I will just wait . . .

There was a time where I would chase the bonefish – the bones – all day, sometimes wading through knee-deep mud, towing a kayak for miles across vast flats. Often I wouldn't see any. What I didn't fully realise then was that it was all about timing or, more specifically, tides. The bonefish know they will be safe from large predators in the 'skinny' water of the flat. Judge the tide right and you can save yourself a lot of hard work and have some great fishing.

My travels in pursuit of bonefish have taken me all over the world: Mexico, Belize, Hawaii, Florida and throughout the Caribbean. I've also fished the atolls of the Indian Ocean in the Seychelles and Maldives. These trips have varied between a week of eight-hour fishing days with a guide to, more typically, shorter sessions squeezed into family holidays. Although, it's always a challenge to find destinations that offer good resort facilities and good bonefishing. Of course, the internet makes life so much easier, and now when Nathalie is planning a holiday, I'm straight on Google Earth looking to see if the particular part of the world she is talking about has any potential for bonefish.

What I'm looking for are flats. These are areas of shallow water typically found in tropical regions. Usually, a Caribbean island will have an ocean side (often to the north), which will have a reef and deep water close to shore, and a more sheltered 'backside' (to the south). For example, the Caicos Bank on the south side of the Turks and Caicos Islands extends for nearly 70 miles towards Haiti and doesn't exceed more than 20 feet in depth for the whole way. Once these shallow banks are found, it's then a matter of zeroing in closer to shore to find the really 'skinny' water. These are areas of mangrove swamp, sandbars or bights that, depending on the tides, can be one or two feet in depth, to completely dry at low tide. They can consist of just a shallow bar of a few hundred yards to expanses of shallows that go on for miles. Of course, bonefish can be found at any depth, but sight-fishing for them with a fly rod requires either wading the shallow flats and looking for signs, such as tailing fish and moving water, or a more hi-tech approach, with a purpose-built shallow-draught flats boat complete with a fish-spotting platform.

Herein lies my addiction: spotting the fish. No matter how many times I do it, seeing a bonefish off in the distance, sunlight glistening off of its exposed tail fin as it burrows into the sand, sets my pulse racing. Then begins the game: how to get in position to make a good cast, taking into account the wind (usually a significant factor on the flats), the position of the sun, and so on. From the minute I spot the fish to (hopefully) the eventual hook-up, I am completely absorbed. Sometimes a shoal of fish will appear out of seemingly nowhere in nine inches of water, heading at speed straight towards you as you frantically try and work a short cast without spooking them. Bonefish seem to be at times almost impossible to spot, as they melt into the bottom. They have not earned their 'ghosts of the flats' reputation for nothing. Many times I've stood, crouching and still, as fish have almost swum through my legs before exploding in panic and shooting off in all directions.

Bonefishing can be challenging in other respects, too. You will spend hours out on the exposed areas of the flats. Sun protection is vitally important, and these days I'm usually well covered up with a UV shirt, a face-protecting snood and plenty of factor 50. I'll carry a backpack with water, energy bars, spare leaders, flies etc . . . Polaroid sunglasses are a must, for eye protection and for fish spotting, cutting through the harsh glare of the tropical conditions. I've also just started to carry a small coarse-fishing 'keep sack' for retaining fish for a photograph. Fishing these wild areas on your own is quite physically demanding.

As well as the wading, a day could involve a long hike over rough ground to reach a particular area, or an hour or two of hard kayaking, sometimes battling headwinds and tides. As far as critters go, the flats are pretty benign. You will see quite a few small stingrays, but a slap of the rod on the water will usually send them on their way. Small sharks prowl the flats also, but in water only a few feet deep there isn't really anything that'll bother you. Venture into slightly deeper water, and you are fair game.

One occasion in the Virgin Islands, I had been fishing a small sand plateau that was bordered on three sides by deeper water and was reputed to be frequented by bones. I had waded all along the bar at low tide looking for tailing fish, but saw nothing. I then resorted to blind casting into the deeper water, wading out up to my waist to achieve a bit more distance. When the tide started to flood back in, I gave up and headed back to my rental car, parked on a bluff, probably 30 feet above where I was fishing. I wearily threw my gear into the boot of the car, and then turned to have one last look out over the area I had been fishing.

I couldn't believe what I saw. A large shark, its chest the size of a beer barrel, was cruising yards from where I had been fishing. As I looked on, somewhat aghast, it dived to the bottom and rubbed its flank against the sand, its gills flaring wildly as it did so. I watched it power off, then made my way, on now slightly wobbly legs, to the car and lowered myself into the driving seat.

You'd think I would have learned my lesson, but a few years later I had a similar occurrence. This time in Nassau, the Bahamas, I was on my own exploring some water out near the airport. I had again waded out into deeper water, up to my midriff, in an effort to reach a tempting spot, when I noticed two large black fins cutting rapidly through the water towards me. It was too late to try to make it back to the shallows so I just stood, not daring to move as they approached. With the rod raised in my right hand, I thought I could at least maybe scare them off if they got too close. I was lucky, as the creatures turned out to be two huge manta rays. Not something you'd want to mess with, but a lot lower on the danger scale than sharks.

I tend to fish for bones on my own these days as I reckon one good fish on my own is worth five with a guide and a fancy boat. My early forays after bonefish were always with guides. The first time was in Andros, Bahamas. We had been working on the album *Powerslave* at Compass Point Studios in Nassau. I'd read about this legendary fish in various saltwater fishing magazines and Andros was a mere hop away from Nassau. The work on the album had progressed well, which was surprising considering some of the stuff we got up to. I'd managed to do some fishing up to that point from the small beach just in front of the studio. I had got hold of some bait, large shrimp, and attached this to a big hook and weight. I then propelled this as far as I could out into the Caribbean. I placed the rod between a couple of rocks and sat back to wait. I'd never been much of a sea-fishing fan, always finding it a bit crude. I was also slightly worried about latching on to something big, angry and with teeth . . . like a particularly ugly moray eel I had seen while snorkelling the day previously.

Just then, the rod top tapped, then drew down slowly. It didn't seem like a bite but I struck anyway, just in case. The feeling coming back up the line was of resistance, yet lifeless, and I continued to wind in. To my right were a couple of condos and now, on the second-floor balcony of the nearest one, a figure in a dressing gown came charging out. Then I saw the rod protruding over said balcony. *Looks like he's in as well.* Dressing-gown man picked up the rod, swept it back expertly and began winding frantically, no doubt already thinking of how he was going to cook this snapper or jack or . . .

We wound and wound until we were facing each other, our lines joined, me Laurel and him Hardy. Hardy turned out to be the late, great Robert Palmer of 'Addicted to Love' fame. I had heard he lived in one of the condos but had never actually seen him. Rumour had it he was completely nocturnal. Anyway, there he was in all his bedroom-attired glory.

He lifted his free arm and waved expansively. 'In all of the Caribbean . . . !' he shouted.

Fair enough, I thought, feeling a right twit. I'd cast over his line. He gave me one more exasperated look before going back inside, shaking his head. Maybe he was in the middle of writing another massive hit when I interrupted him.

A few years later plans were made for a quick trip to Andros. Nathalie flew out to join me for the three-day break. I'd found a small hotel that also offered bonefish guides and soon we were settled in our island paradise – except it wasn't. As is wont to happen in the Caribbean, I woke up to find that there was no guide available that day. Maybe tomorrow? The weather also wasn't cooperating, with high winds and scudding clouds. Nathalie and I made the best of it, pluckily holding on to our lounge chairs on the small beach to prevent the now howling wind blowing us back to Nassau.

The next morning, as I lay awake with one eye open, I heard . . . silence. We had dozed off to the sound of wind rattling the windows but now as I drew the curtains it was a perfect tropical day.

Things got even better at breakfast when I was informed that the hotel had found me a guide for the day.

'The rev'rend will pick you up right after breakfast, sir.'

'Great! Thanks,' I replied.

Nathalie and I looked at each other. *Reverend?* we mouthed silently.

The 'Rev' Rollo was 85 if he was a day. A short man with still powerful arms and a huge belly, he sat now in the driver's seat of a dilapidated 4x4 truck. We piled in. We greeted him enthusiastically and were met with a barely discernible nod of the head. The solemn expression unchanging, we lapsed into an uncomfortable silence.

As we made our way over the roads, alternating between tarmac and rough track, we would pass the odd local. The same barely imperceptible nod of the head would be exchanged. Seemed like everybody knew everybody. Sensing our curiosity, at the next exchange, the Rev volunteered 'Brudda.' He then said, 'Sister.' A little further on, 'Brudda-in-law.' We were beginning to get the picture. Meanwhile, every half-mile or so was marked by a plane wreck. We must have seen 20 or so. Drug runners. You could almost feel the Rev's contempt as we passed the rusting Cessnas.

Eventually, after navigating a particularly bum-breaking track, we arrived at a small dock where the Rev's boat was moored. Thankfully it was a sturdy-looking craft with a decent-looking motor. It did not, however, have a lookout platform, standard in most flats boats and essential for spotting bones on the flat. Ah well, he was an old boy and we were lucky to get him. I think I would have felt bad anyway, with him poling me for miles.

Usually at this point, your guide will commence an essential conversation regarding tactics for the day, size of fish that were expected to be encountered, and so on. Not so the Rev. Before I could say 'Crazy Charlie', he had unwedged himself from the seat and was outside the car. I watched him pick up a rock and wedge it under the front wheel, then make his way slowly, oh so slowly, down to the boat. He spent a while readying the boat, then motioned to us to join him. We eagerly clambered aboard, Nathalie with *Vanity Fair* and sun cream, me with a 7-weight and a spring in my step. I thought I caught a slight frown when the Rev saw the fly rod, or should I say his permanent frown deepened slightly? No matter, it was a beautiful Caribbean day and I was going to catch my first bonefish.

I love the flats, and I was full of anticipation when we were cruising out that morning. A while later, we came to a stop by some mangroves on the edge of a large flat, sandy at its edges, giving way to seagrass further out. Classic bones country. I readied myself, slapping on some more factor 50 and stuffing my pockets with forceps, fly boxes and so on.

'We'll be wading then?' I enquired.

'No,' he said, gravely. 'They will come.'

I sat down slowly. The Rev delved into an old bucket full of mashed-up crabs and conch. He then proceeded to bait the sandy shelf. After a few minutes some small jacks appeared and darted around in front of us, excited by the bait. This was the Rev's cue. He reached down and grabbed two spinning-type rods with fixed spool reels, then handed one to Nathalie and one to me.

'Get ready,' he instructed.

Sure enough, a bonefish appeared. I excitedly lobbed my baited hook into the path of the fish. At the sound of the bait hitting the water, the bone accelerated towards the tasty morsel and gobbled it immediately. On feeling the resistance, it took off across the flat, the line sizzling from the reel. Eventually, after two more powerful runs, we brought the fish aboard. A nice one, around 4lb: my first bonefish. Not on the fly, but still . . .

After a quick photo I went to return the fish to fight another day and all that.

'No!' boomed the Rev. 'It's a sin to put them back!'

I'd already worked out that this wasn't the kind of trip that you see pictured in glossy fishing magazines, the kind where all the anglers are dressed in state-of-the-art fishing garb, holding 10lb bonefish and smiling, all perfect teeth. No, this was the Rev's watch, so we just went with it. I handed him the fish, which he chucked unceremoniously into an old cooler.

The Rev said that he sent the fish over to the orphanage in Nassau. No problem with that, and the four-pounder was joined with another half a dozen fish by lunchtime. The flesh of a bonefish is reputedly very tasty but, as the name implies, the many bones make preparation difficult. The locals get around this by first boiling the fish then separating the flaky white meat. They finally pound it out for fear of any remaining bones and mould it into fishcakes.

Meanwhile on the weather front, things were not looking good. A bad squall was gathering on the horizon and we decided to head back. We were almost back to the dock when the Rev sprung his biggest surprise. Suddenly the boat's engine stopped and, with a huge splash, the Rev fell backwards into the water. Understandably panicked, Nat and I rushed to his assistance but we were too late: there was no sign of the Reverend.

'Jeez. He must've had a bloody heart attack, poor old bugger!'
I cried.

'Maybe you should dive in?' said Nat.

'It's the Caribbean, full of bloody sharks . . .'

I was interrupted by a huge exhalation of air as the Rev
surfaced clutching a large lobster. The crustacean was thrown
into the boat and the Rev took a huge gulp of air and dived
down once more.

'What the fuck? It's a lobster!'

'I know what it is!'

I managed to grab the understandably upset lobster and
wrestle it into the cooler, at which point, the Rev reappeared.
This time an even larger lobster was lobbed into the boat. The
Rev then pulled himself up over the side and into the boat in
one fluid motion like a 20-year-old. He resumed position at the
helm. Nathalie and I looked at each other and burst out laughing. The Reverend was finally smiling.

We ended up back at the Reverend's house, waiting for a lift
back to the hotel. The old 4x4 had broken down. No doubt it
would be running again soon and there would be someone in
the family, brother, cousin or whoever, who was good with
engines.

Now we sat in the front room with the Rev and his wife,
slightly uncomfortable in the silence of the evening. They
weren't much for small talk, content to sit and stare at nothing
in particular. Of course, we tried to move things along,
commenting on family photos, the weather, and so on. But the

conversation was stilted to say the least. Not rude on their part, just their way. Eventually our lift arrived, we said our goodbyes and I handed a bundle of dollar bills to the Rev, who accepted them without a word . . .

The next day was warm and settled but unfortunately we were flying back to Nassau. The flight wasn't until late afternoon so we decided to have lunch in the small terrace above the beach at the hotel before we left. Before we had time to order our food, plates were brought to the table, followed by lobster salad.

'The Reverend's granddaughter came by the hotel with this for you this morning. Enjoy!' said the waiter.

The lobster salad was delicious and we toasted the Reverend with ice-cold St Pauli Girl beers. 'It's a sin to put 'em back! Cheers!'

Back at Compass Point Nassau we continued working on what was to become the album *Powerslave*. With the bulk of the work done, it was time for overdubs. Dave Murray and I would do alternative sessions, tracking solos with producer Martin Birch. We were all slightly in awe of Martin when we first started working with him on the *Killers* album in 1980. After all, he'd been responsible for production on all the records that had inspired us in the 1970s: Sabbath, Blue Oyster Cult and, of course, a string of albums by Deep Purple.

Martin was an excellent engineer and a hands-on producer. He also had an aura of quiet authority about him, enhanced not least by the fact he was a judo blackbelt. We worked hard and played hard in those days. A productive recording session was followed by an evening of 'relaxation'. This usually started with one of the assistant local engineers mixing up the margaritas. Feet would be put up on the mixing desk and the 'relaxing' would ensue.

The drink flowed. Stories were told. Much laughter would be had. Almost inevitably at some point in the evening (probably around 4am) Martin would feel the need to practise his karate moves. Roadies would scramble to defend precious guitars on stands from Martin's swishing kicks and chops. Others in the know would move slowly into various nooks and crannies. Sometimes an impromptu jam would ensue. God, I hope someone taped over them.

After one such night, I staggered off to my bed as the sun was coming up. I chuckled to myself. A good few days' work done, a bit over the top tonight, but I knew there would be no work tomorrow. I drifted off to sleep, dreaming of a lie-in, a snapper for lunch and a kip on the beach.

It was only a few hours later, 10am, that the phone rang.

'Morning, dear boy!' It was Martin. 'Let's crack on with those overdubs!'

'Er, yeah, OK. Give me an hour,' I croaked.

My brain was banging. I felt like not only had I drunk a pitcher of margarita but someone had hit me over the head with it. Coffee and calories were forced down, shades were placed carefully on, Ibuprofen swallowed. I made my way to the studio, a short walk down the hill from the condos – a swanky development complete with palm trees and swimming pool, separated from the shanty town next door by a high, chain-link fence.

I felt dizzy but when Martin wanted to work, you turned up. He produced 'Highway Star' for Christ's sake!

I made my way through the studio and into the control room. Martin was sitting behind the desk, bright-eyed and bushy-tailed, and next to him was Robert Palmer. (Martin hadn't been to bed yet. I found out later that he had knocked on Robert's door in the small hours and Palmer had broken out the rum.) Bloody hell. This was getting worse.

'Morning, Adrian. This is Robert.'

Robert smiled and we shook hands. 'Have we met before?' said Robert, his head tilting slightly.

'Er, I don't think so,' I lied.

They were still drinking and Robert was in his dressing gown and a cravat. Suave.

'What do you fancy?' said Martin.

'Bit early for me,' I replied.

'No. Which track do you want to have a go at first?'

'Oh, "Powerslave".'

'Right-o.'

No pressure then. I disappeared into the kitchen for a much-needed coffee. I was in a state. The combination of lack of sleep, nerves and an increasingly severe hangover had resulted in a mild case of the shakes.

I've never considered myself a virtuoso, able to produce reams of shredding solos at the drop of a hat. I have a pretty good melodic sense and I tended in those days to work out a lot of my solos before recording sessions. I used to see this as a bit of a failing on my part until, years later, I read a story about Eric Clapton having to halt a session on a Richie Sambora track that he was guesting on so he could go off on his own to work something out.

I gathered myself in the kitchen. I had a few ideas for the solo section so, loins girded, I returned to the control room. I picked up my guitar, an Ibanez 1 Pickup Roadster, and nodded to Martin to run the track. As the tape hissed rewind, I caught the eye of my roadie Marcus, partner-in-crime during the previous night's revelry. Guitar techs have to perform many duties, from technical wizardry to Agony Aunt, and Marcus, sadly no longer with us, was one of the best. His eyes said it all. *Go for it, mate!*

Martin rolled the tape. The section I had to play over was an up-tempo piece coming out of Dave's dreamy Hendrix-inspired middle section. The slow piece ends with a two-bar build-up into my solo. Martin increased the volume at this point, and the music roared out of the huge wall-mounted speakers in the control room. The idea was to create an atmosphere of performance and most overdubbing is done this way, with the musician and recording staff in the same room. Guitar amps are isolated and mic'd up in a separate studio nicknamed the 'War Room' because the volume of the speakers is akin to being under bombardment. Usually I can't even listen to music when I'm hungover, let alone play, but I was on the spot. I threw myself into the solo. Shit or bust. Not my usual style.

'Fuckin' great,' said Palmer. He seemed genuinely impressed.

'Yeah well, you know . . .' I feigned nonchalance.

I did a few more takes but, as is often the case, none were as good as the first. Martin decided to call it a day. I could see he was starting to get a bit creased around the edges. I put down my guitar and prepared to say my goodbyes.

'Good work, mate,' said Palmer, extending a hand. 'I'm sure we've met before.' Then it clicked. 'You cast over my line!'

'Yeah, sorry about that.'

He had the good grace to laugh.

He seemed like a good bloke and, although he was from a slightly different musical genre, I respected what he had achieved in the biz. Hopefully, after that day it was mutual. He probably didn't think much of my casting skills though . . .

EPILOGUE

When I open my eyes again, it takes me a second to remember where we are. Ah yes. Mexico City, 2019. The Legacy of the Beast tour. The sirens of our police escort have stopped blaring because we have arrived at the venue. As usual, our head security guy, Jeff Weir, is on hand to cast a protective eye over proceedings and show us the way to the dressing rooms. The support band are on stage; they'll be giving their all, sweating over every note. But all you can hear backstage is the almighty rumble of the bottom end as it passes through the structure of the building. The venues we play nowadays are usually sports arenas, built for viewing and not for sound quality. But hey, you do your best.

In the past, the backstage area would be full of all manner of rock 'n' roll humanity. Groupies, drug dealers, record company employees, radio DJs and hangers-on would make the journey to the dressing rooms. Their presence would be sometimes hazardous and usually draining. Nowadays, backstage is for friends and family only and we save 100 per cent for the show. Nathalie and I make our way unmolested to the catering area. Hungry or not, I'll have a quick bite to eat, making sure I have energy for the gig. We wander over to the buffet, pile a few items on our plates, then find somewhere to sit. I say hello to various crew members. I nod to a table full of guys who I see from time to time, riggers or truck drivers most likely. They sport various T-shirts of tours past — miles logged like badges of honour. It occurs to me that our travelling circus is so big, I don't know everyone by name. In terms of familiarity, it's the backline crew, those in charge of our amps, guitars and drums, the band are closest to. Enter Sean Brady, my guitar tech. I'd told our tour manager earlier that I wanted to speak to him before the show. He makes his way across the room, his usually jovial aura shrouded now slightly by concern. Maybe he thinks I wasn't happy with last night's show, or I have a list of technical adjustments for him to make to my equipment.

'Everything all right, mate?' he enquires in broad Brummie.

'Yeah fine, mate. By the way, great show the other night. Spot on!'
I say.

'Monitors all right?'

'Yeah, great.'

'Guitars OK?'

'Yeah, no problem.'

His mood brightens. 'Day off tomorrow,' he says.

'Yep,' I reply.

'You want your fishing gear off the truck, don't you?'

'Yep.'

Tomorrow we'll be in another country, city, hotel. Maybe, there will be a lake or river close by. Another adventure to log into my memory, another monster waiting in the river as I continue my journey in rock.

ACKNOWLEDGEMENTS

I would like to thank, in no particular order, Dave Shack, Mary Henry, Nathalie Dufresne-Smith, Dave Daniel, Patrick Smith.

GLOSSARY

Arlesey Bomb: Angling weight designed to assist with casting a long distance.

Bank stick: Extendable poles pointed on one end used to hold threaded bite alarms and rod rests which cradle their rods.

Barbules: Characteristic whiskers on certain breeds of fish, i.e. carp, which are used to search for food.

Bivvied-up: Camping in a small domed tent to keep sheltered.

Blind casting: Casting for fish in places where they habitually go, rather than depending on visual cues.

Boilies: Form of bait packed with nutrients and attractants to draw a carp in.

Buzzer: Another word for a bite alarm.

Caster: Chrysalis stage of a maggot, used to attract larger fish.

Centrepin: Typical type of fishing reel with a line around a single spool, sometimes with bearings.

Deadbait: Dead fish used to catch predatory fish such as pike and perch.

Delkims: Brand of fish buzzing alarm used by carp anglers.

Drop-shot rig: A small thin-wire hook with a weight attached to the tag end of the line, allowing the bait to be kept off the bottom.

Dry fly: Artificial fly that mimics insects that float on the water's surface.

End / Terminal tackle: Generic description for any gear that attaches to the end of a rod making direct contact with the fish.

Floating-crust method: Using bait such as bread or dog/cat biscuits (or artificial versions).

Groundbait: Balls of various natural ingredients, such as fish-meal or breadcrumbs, blended together and thrown into the water to attract carp.

Heli-fishing: Abbreviation of helicopter-fishing.

Keepnet: A tube net that holds fish so they can be weighed (if in a contest) or simply viewed at the end of a day's fishing.

Legering: Keeping bait held on the river bottom by means of a weight or feeder, rather than with a float.

Nymphs: Artificial flies that imitate the underwater larva-form of flies; used to catch trout in particular.

Match fishing: Contest between various anglers.

Mending: Using a rod to pick up and reposition a line against the current to perfectly present flies as bait with the minimum of drag.

Method feeder: Open feeder for ground bait or pellets where the bait sits on top of the feed.

Mono: Abbreviation of monofilament fishing line; one made from a single fibre of plastic.

Pop-ups: Abbreviation of popped-up baits which are often a bright colour to attract fish – such as pineapple yellow or pink.

Peg: Station used by an angler during match fishing – from the wooden pegs used to demarcate them.

Quiver tip: Flexible and sensitive extension on a fishing rod that indicates when the fish has taken the bait.

Riffle: Shallow piece of land in a flowing channel, such as a river – organisms fish eat gather there, so fish wait nearby.

Roach or **Match pole**: Very long flexible fishing poles used since Victorian times to catch roach.

Rod blanks: Basic part of a custom-made fishing rod used for fly fishing.

Rubber shad imitation: Soft plastic bait that imitates live prey in the water.

Running rig: Direct connection between the main line, rig and the hook which confuses carp and prevents them from shaking the hook loose.

Skinny water: Another name for shallow water.

Slab: a specimen common bream (slang).

Slack water: Short period when a tidal river is not moving in either direction.

Snag fishing: Fishing up against or near heavy cover such as fallen trees.

Split shot: Small pellet of metal that add weights to the fishing line.

Spod: Bait-filled rocket with a buoyant nose that releases feed downwards into the water.

Spomb: Bait-dispensing device like the **spod**, with special fins for accuracy of casting.

Streamer: An artificial fly, also known as a wet fly, or 'Woolly Bugger', which represents a baitfish.

Swim: Designated area that can be fished from a **peg**.

INDEX

AS indicates Adrian Smith.

AC/DC 97, 160
Ahr River, Germany 242–3
Alpine Valley, Wisconsin 18–20
Andros Island, Bahamas
    264–71
Arnold River, New Zealand
    112–15
Avon River, Hampshire 21–4,
    29, 136, 242

Bahamas 107, 194, 264–75
Banff, Canada 80–3
barbel 21–9, 33–40, 44, 47, 49,
    50–1, 95, 136, 189, 192, 238,
    245–58
Barnett, Andy 31–2, 228
Barry, John 8, 10
bass 18, 19, 57–8, 60–1, 65, 66–7,
    69, 72–6; largemouth 57,
    61, 66, 69; peacock 66–7,
    72–6; smallmouth 76
Bayley, Blaze 168
bears 82–3, 87, 90–1, 115–16, 236
Big Jim Lake, Tasmania 129–32
Birch, Martin 271–5

Bois de Boulogne, Paris 137,
    164–7, 169–73, 174–5,
    176–9
Bonaparte Provincial Park,
    Canada 83, 85–91
bonefish 66, 106, 116, 117,
    159–60, 260–4, 266–9
Bowler, Martin 202, 250, 252
Bowley, Martin 230–3
Bow River, Alberta 80–1
Boyer Leisure 25, 136
Brady, Sean 244, 277–8
bream 3, 24, 37–8, 44, 94, 95,
    136, 141, 144, 145, 151, 166,
    182, 183, 184, 186, 188, 192,
    193, 197, 198, 203, 209, 217,
    246
Brunner, Lake, New Zealand
    111–17
Burr, Clive 18, 19, 53–4, 55

Campuzano, Eduardo 234, 235,
    236
Canada 47, 80–96, 100–3, 124n,
    155–62, 185, 196

carp 7–8, 10–11, 17, 18–20, 24, 25, 34–5, 36, 40, 47, 49, 57, 59, 60, 65, 66, 76, 135–41, 164–79, 181–99, 202, 203, 204, 208, 211–14, 217, 220, 221, 222–3, 224, 226, 227, 232–3, 245–6, 257–8; mirror carp 7, 8, 135–6, 170–3, 193, 208, 211, 246
catfish 76, 160, 166, 178, 220
Cedar Lodge, South Island, New Zealand 117–28
Central Park, New York 56–8, 60–2
China 204, 239–40
chub 21–2, 23, 24, 25, 28, 34, 36, 37, 38–9, 41–51, 115, 135, 136, 139–40, 238, 247, 249
Clapton, East London 2, 3, 9, 14, 31, 32, 42, 91
Collingham, Nottinghamshire 247–58
Collins, John 205–6
Colne, River 24, 26, 34, 47–51, 135–6, 137–41
Compass Point, Bahamas 107, 194, 264, 271–5
Conningbrook, Kent 256–8
Connolly, Martin 'Hippy Martin' 224–7
Copacabana Palace Hotel, Rio 97
Cundiff, Julian 213

Day, Ian 158, 234
Deep Purple 13–14, 202, 271
Devils Lane Lake, Surrey 203

Dickinson, Bruce 68, 98, 99, 100, 107, 167, 168, 187, 244
Dufresne, Carl 185
Dufresne, Marc 157, 239
Dufresne, Quottnim 157, 239

Ebro River, Spain 34–5, 220–2, 225–7
El Salvador 204–5
Étang de Longchamp, Paris 172–3
Everglades, Florida 66, 69, 70–1

Falls mall, Florida 68, 71
Florida 63–76, 263
Fox Mere, Essex 246
Fraser, Dick 118–19, 121, 125, 128
Fraser River, Canada 155–6, 158–62

Gallagher, Liam 149
Germany 242–3, 245
Gers, Janick 148, 149, 168
Gorham, Scott 227, 229–32
Gramercy Park Hotel, New York 54–5
Grand Union Canal, London 3–4, 5, 9, 141, 144–6, 148, 150–3
Greynolds Park, Miami 72–6
Grey River, New Zealand 113
gudgeon 5, 116, 161

Hackney Marshes, London 2–3, 13
Harris, Steve 32, 33, 107, 108, 149, 195

Hawkwind 15–16
Hearn, Bob 83, 85, 86, 87, 89
heli-fishing 118
Hong Kong 108, 111
Hunter River, New Zealand
    124–8
Hynde, Chrissie 228, 229

India 105, 108–11, 224–5
Iron Maiden xi, 32; *A Matter of
    Life and Death* tour 47; AS
    hiatus from 24, 46, 167–8;
    AS joins 17–18, 32–3; AS
    re-joins 47, 167–8; Boeing
    757/Ed Force One 187–8,
    201–2, 204–5, 206, 238–9;
    Brave New World 167, 168–9,
    175; *Dance of Death* 143–4;
    Eddie mascot, AS on 202;
    'If Eternity Should Fail'
    244; *Killers* tour 53–4, 64,
    123, 271; *Legacy of the Beast*
    tour xi, 56, 63, 64–5, 67–8,
    76, 214, 277–8; *Matter of
    the Beast* tour 48; *Powerslave*
    69, 107, 266, 273–4; Rock
    in Rio festivals, Brazil
    (1985) 96–9; *Somewhere Back
    in Time* tour 155–7, 187–8,
    233–4; *Somewhere in Time*
    103, 106, 107–8, 123, 124;
    'Stranger in a Strange Land'
    123–4, 124*n*; *The Book of
    Souls* 175–6; *The Book of
    Souls* tour 204–5, 213,
    238–45, 260; *The Final*

Frontier 194–5; *The Final
    Frontier tour* 195, 201–2; *The
    Number of the Beast* 18;
    World Slavery Tour 69–70,
    77–8, 84–5, 91, 96–100

Jersey 107–8
Judas Priest 55, 64

Kamloops, Canada 83–4, 85–91
Kashmir, India 109–11
Kennet, River 25, 26–9, 136
King, Lawrence 247, 250, 252,
    253, 254, 255, 257, 258
Kings Weir fishery 44–5
Kiske, Michael: *Instant
    Clarity* 167
Korda Lake, Colne Valley 204,
    206–12, 214–17, 245

Lea, River 32, 41, 44, 94
Lee Navigation 2, 3, 5, 9
Lewis, 'Big' Dave 188
Liedeman, Gary 228
London Lakes, Tasmania 128–33

Macey, Dean 247, 248, 250, 251,
    252, 253, 254, 255, 257, 258
manatee 73–4
Manchester United 12, 17
McBrain, Nicko 98, 228
McLaughlin, Dave 14, 15, 16
Mequinenza, Spain 220–2, 225
Miami, Florida 63–76
Michigan, Lake 58–60
Millstream 41–2, 51

Milton Pan lake, Kent 202–3
Murray, Dave 14, 15–16, 18, 19, 32, 33, 43, 54, 70, 79, 156, 228, 244, 271, 274

Nassau, Bahamas 194, 264–6, 271–5
Newman, Gary 204
New Orleans, Louisiana 128
New York 53–7, 58–62, 84, 85, 96, 99–100, 107
New Zealand 105, 106, 108, 111–28, 129, 175, 240–2

Oasis 148–9, 153
Ojeda, Eddie 85
Okeechobee, Lake, Florida 66
Orient, Lake of the, France 213–14

Palmer, Robert 265–6, 273–5
Paris, France 137, 163–71, 173, 174–5, 176–9, 194–5
Peck, Darrell 213–14
perch 3, 10, 11, 24, 67
pike 94, 95, 141, 144–7, 148, 150–3, 175, 238
Pits, The, Stanstead Abbotts, Hertfordshire 8–11, 13–14, 20, 184
Psycho Motel 167

Queen 97, 98, 99
Queensryche 99
Quito, Ecuador 234–6

Reading, Northern California 71–2
Redfern, Mike (Spug) 57, 245–7, 248–9, 250, 251, 252–3, 254, 256–7
Richards, Keith 55, 78
roach 3–4, 5, 10, 11, 14, 17, 24, 94, 115, 145, 151, 165, 166, 186, 232, 238
Robertson, Brian 227–8
Rollo, Reverend 266–71
Rourke, Mickey 54–5

salmon 93, 94, 101, 156, 160, 237, 242
Scorpions 18, 19, 20
Second World War 2, 94, 133
Shaw, Bernie 227–8
Sheep Walk, Shepperton 203
Shirley, Kevin 149, 168
Skitchine Lodge, Canada 83, 85–91, 94
Smallwood, Rod 99, 167
Smith, Adrian: ASAP album 82; boat, buys 144–8, 150, 151, 153; Bruce Dickinson solo projects and 167; childhood 2–13, 21–4, 41–5, 51; depression 46–7; family *see individual family member name*; fishing *see individual place and fish species name*; football and 12–13, 37, 185; Iron Maiden and *see* Iron Maiden; music career, birth of 13–17; practice routine

262; Psycho Motel 167; 'The Final Frontier' and 195; travel *see individual place name*; The Untouchables 185–6; Urchin and 31–3, 97, 188, 228; 'Wasted Years' and 6, 108–9

Smith, Dylan (son) 185, 186, 232–6, 244

Smith, Fred (father) 3–4, 5–6, 8, 9–10, 14, 23, 42, 44, 45, 232

Smith, Kathleen (mother) 2, 5

Smith, Nathalie (wife) 103, 228, 229, 239, 279; AM first meets 79–80; engagement to AS 111; travel/fishing trips with AS 71, 72, 82, 83, 86, 88, 90–1, 92–4, 96, 101, 102, 103, 105–6, 108, 110, 111, 113, 115, 119, 122, 125, 127, 128, 131, 132, 261, 266, 268, 270, 277

Smith, Patrick (brother) 3, 9, 10, 11, 12, 220–4, 225

snakes 70–2, 75, 130, 131–2

South Muskham Fishery, Nottinghamshire 245–7

Srinagar, India 109–11

Stan, Uncle 41–4, 51

Studio Guillaume Tell, Paris 167, 175, 176

sturgeon 155–62

Suresnes, the Pond of (l'étang de Suresnes), Paris 163–71, 173, 174–5, 176–9

Tasmania 128–33

Tasmanian devil 132–3

Taylor Lake, Canada 82–3

tench xi, 34, 38, 44, 166, 182, 184–99, 202–4, 209, 211, 212, 213, 214, 215–17, 245, 246

Test, River 230–2

Thames, River 5, 34–40

Thin Lizzy 227–30

Tolpits Lake, Hertfordshire 186–7, 188–94

Tottenham Locks, London 5–6, 9, 161

Trent, River 237–8, 245–59

trout 23, 71, 79–80, 81, 82, 83, 86, 88, 89, 90, 91, 93–4, 96, 106, 109, 110, 112–21, 126–7, 128, 129, 130, 131, 151, 156, 230, 231, 234, 235, 236, 242, 243; blue trout 231; brown trout 80, 106, 113, 117, 126, 131, 242; rainbow trout 89, 93–4, 113, 121, 125, 235, 236, 242–3

Turks and Caicos Islands 159, 259–63

Twisted Sister 84–5

Untouchables, The 185–6

Urchin 31–3, 97, 188, 228

Vancouver, British Columbia 103, 155–8

Virgin Islands 263–4

Wacken Festival 206, 245
Wellington Country Park,
    Berkshire 186
Wells Gray Provincial Park,
    Canada 91–6
Whitesnake 97, 98, 99

Wilson, John 27, 49,
    146, 147
Wraysbury, Berkshire 196–9

Young River, New Zealand
    119–21